It Didn't Start with Me But It Stops with Me

Ten Days of Deliverance prayers that will set you, your family and your generation free

It's time to live life abundantly

By
Miriam Matthews

Dedication

I dedicate this book to my children, Zamaria, Ava, Jesse, and Noah. You inspire me to be who I am today and to keep growing. I am so thankful that God chose me to be your mother and blessed me with you all. I treasure you and I pray that you are triumphant and successful in everything you do. The blessings of the Lord are upon you. May you always walk under an open heaven!

"For the person I was when I started writing this book, and the person I am now."

Foreword

It Didn't Start with Me, But It Stops with Me, by Coach Miriam Matthews is a powerful read that has the potential to ignite your faith and cause you to walk in boldness using your authority in Jesus Christ. Miriam Matthews is a true prophet of the Lord, and this book is anointed by God to give prayer strategies for the common areas of our lives in which the enemy tries to bind us.

Miriam received a powerful revelation from John 10:10: the enemy comes to steal, kill, and destroy, but Jesus came to give life much more abundantly. This revelation further mandates her assignment from heaven that this book is God sent. The righteous are bold as a lion.

I have observed Miriam over the years and know firsthand that she is passionate about prayer and intercession. She strives to please God and she loves His people. She constantly serves and helps so many people get free and delivered. Through each chapter, she openly shares her vulnerabilities because she doesn't want anyone to experience what she endured. She has also gained experience in helping to set the captives free.

It Didn't Start with Me, But It Stops with Me is a powerful tool that should be in every home. It's not just a book; it's a practical guide for the spiritual battles we all face – light versus darkness and flesh versus Spirit. This book shows us how to conduct warfare effectively and gain the confidence to not be afraid of the enemy or ignorant of his devices.

Miriam has strategically authored prayers that will help us get free from mental bondage. The mind is where the enemy tries to attack us, and cause us to doubt God and who we are in Him. God instructed Miriam Matthews to also tackle areas such as identity, our emotions, relationships, health, and the ability to persevere. Miriam has prayed these prayers herself, allowing her to break free in many areas of her life. This book holds the potential for us to break free from these chains as well and live a life of freedom and victory.

I recommend using this tool for a ten-day journey. The preparation time is to renew your mind and renounce any demonic patterns and curses you may have come into agreement with (intentionally or in ignorance). Then, on days 1 through 10, you learn the background of each topic and how to win over the situation through strategic teaching and prayer declarations. Take notes while reading, highlight things that stand out to you, and use a bookmark as a placeholder while you commit to your ten-day journey to freedom.

After you finish the book, leave a review on Amazon or another retailer's website on how much this book has blessed you. Do share with others this excellent book that God has used to break demonic strongholds in your life.

Prophetess Kimberly Moses

Table of Contents

Introduction

Congratulations on accepting the call to cut the enemy out of your life and that of your family! You are breaking chains that have been in your bloodline and those around you! Additionally, you are ensuring that those that come after you will be free as well! John 10:10 says, "The thief does not come except to steal, and to kill, and to destroy. I have come that they may have life, and that they may have *it* more abundantly."

A thief is one who is good at concealing that he has been stealing, killing, or creating destruction. Often, by the time we are aware of it, the damage has already been done. Why is this? Because the thief does announce his entry. He comes stealthily into your home, and your marriage, around your children, your finances, your health, your businesses aiming to destroy it so that you are discouraged, depressed, and defeated. He ultimately wants you to die along with the dreams that God has given you.

How did John 10:10 come up? I remember seeing this recurring number 10:10 on the clock over and over again. I'm not talking about any new age practice, or seeking out numbers in order to understand something from the universe. I'm talking about God meeting me where I was, and speaking in a variety of ways, whether they be dreams, visions, and even numbers. I kept seeing the number 1010 and every time I would see it, I sensed that He was telling me that there was a thief that was coming or had already come. As I began to put the pieces together, immediately my hands covered the top of my head, as I had this profound moment of realization!

I realized that's why my husband and I kept fighting, instead of fighting the enemy in prayer to either prevent what was going to happen or be the catalyst for change. I would attack those around me instead of attacking the thief, the enemy. I allowed anger to control me instead of controlling it. I allowed the fear of rejection to make me so defensive to the point of arguing over and over again. I let the fear of being vulnerable or rejected hold me back from learning how to communicate in a healthy way.

I was weighed down with these issues, as if something were holding me, hindering me, and oppressing me. These were strongholds set up by enemy. This was impacting my business and the financial liberty I was supposed to have until the thief was exposed and evicted along with the spirit of rejection. My friend, the enemy is here to create a hold on you and your children too so that you are hindered and stuck in a vicious cycle.

Let's be clear that there is an enemy operating against you and me. He opposes us because he doesn't want us to prosper. Therefore, he plants seeds of discouragement, confusion, and chaos in you and your family. He wants you all to bicker and argue with each other. He wants to divide your household, confuse your identity, and be in poverty.

When did all that happen? These seeds were planted before you were even born. Many of the things that you're dealing with now didn't even start with you. However, as the title of this book says, it's going to stop with you. That enemy that crept in generations ago has been following your bloodline to the point that it wants you and everything around you destroyed. Whether you have children or not, it is imperative that you use it to guide you to take back what the enemy has stolen by force.

The way you take it back begins with understanding not just who you are but *whose* you are. You belong to King Jesus and He has already defeated the enemy. Therefore, everything you do from now on is based on the truth that the battle has already been won by Jesus. However, you still have to enforce the victory. You have to use your mind and your mouth as a weapon of mass destruction against the enemy. Proverbs 18:21 tells us that death and life is in the power of your tongue. The enemy does not want you to know the power and authority invested in you. But I am exposing the enemy for who he is because he has stolen from you long enough.

I want you to say with me, "Enough is enough!" Say it again, "Enough is enough!" Now say, "It didn't start with me but it stops with me." Say it one more time! "It didn't start with me, but it stops with me!"

That's right, get hyped. Get ready. It's time to kick hell out of your house and allow Heaven over you and in your house.

Look at John 10:10 again: *"The thief comes not but to steal, kill and destroy but I have come that you may have life and life more abundantly."* So now you're stopping the enemy mentioned in the first part of the verse and entering into the manifestation of the abundant life that God promises in the second part.

You have the full backing of Heaven. I'm reminded of the time when Elisha the prophet was about to be attacked by the Syrian army. Elisha knew that heaven was going to back him up and had full confidence in the God of armies. He knew the benefits of being a child of God. He understood that warfare is spiritual and what you see physically has already happened spiritually.

As Elisha was preparing for the attack, he was physically surrounded by the enemy's army but he was spiritually surrounded by the angelic army of the Lord. His servant was dismayed and said, "How will we win?"

Elisha asked God, *"Lord, I pray, open his eyes that he may see."*

Then the Lord opened the eyes of the young man, and he saw. And behold, the mountain was full of horses and chariots of fire all around Elisha. (2 Kings 6:17)

Many times, we're on the defensive where we are reacting to what is happening in the physical, and we begin to fight each other. We become so discouraged about our relationships, finances, children, jobs, health – you name it – that we become depleted and defeated. However, it's time to get on the offensive by realizing who you are and who backs you up.

Like Elisha, you have a great number of angels that are surrounding you spiritually. Right now, I want you to ask God to open your spiritual eyes to see and understand the depths of His love for you, and the protection and resources He has already assigned to you spiritually. I remember, when God began to open my spiritual eyes, He was showing me not only the enemy but the angels that surrounded me as well. Yes, real encounters! How amazing is that? These angels were fighting as I was praying, and they were bringing my prayers to the throne room of Heaven, so God could answer them.

As I began to understand how to war spiritually, I began to see things shift within my home, my marriage, my children, my finances, my businesses, my health, and everything concerning me. I began to experience the victory! However, the victory started with my participation in a war that was already set up to work in my favor. Yes, go ahead and start clapping because this war is set up to work in your favor too! But you must fight according to the manual of instructions God has given in His word.

Invitation to receive Jesus Christ: For those who are new to the faith and have not yet received Jesus Christ as their Lord and Savior, it is essential to invite Him into your heart before embarking on the journey of deliverance and praying the prayers in this book. By accepting Christ, you receive the Holy Spirit, who empowers you to experience true freedom and transformation. Below is a prayer you can say to begin this relationship with Him:---

Prayer of Salvation: "Dear Heavenly Father, I come to You today with an open heart, acknowledging that I need You in my life. I confess that I have sinned and fallen short of Your glory. I believe that You sent Your Son, Jesus Christ, to die on the cross for my sins, and that He rose again on the third day, conquering sin and death.

Today, I choose to turn away from my sins and invite Jesus into my heart as my Lord and Savior. I believe that through His sacrifice, I am forgiven, cleansed, and made new. I surrender my life to You and ask for Your Holy Spirit to fill me, guide me, and empower me to live according to Your will.

Thank You, Lord, for saving me, for setting me free, and for giving me eternal life. I commit my life to You and trust in Your promises. In Jesus' name, I pray. Amen."

The Power of Intercession

Intercessory work is powerful. As an intercessor, you are standing in the gap, and praying on behalf of others who are lost or deep in sin. Unless you cover them in prayer, they may not receive the deliverance, breakthrough, or salvation they need. Your prayers have the ability to shift things not only in your own life but in the lives of those for whom you intercede. Therefore, what you say in prayer can literally save, set free, and deliver others, as you are acting as a spiritual advocate on their behalf. This vital role is a calling to partner with God in bringing His mercy, healing, and restoration to those around you. Here is a breakdown of why intercessory work is so powerful.

First, God has designated a specific role for the intercessor, as seen in Ezekiel 22:30, where He sought someone to stand in the gap for the land. Without an intercessor, judgment follows, but with one pleading to God on their behalf, mercy can prevail. This illustrates that intercession is not just an optional part of spiritual life — it is essential for others to receive God's intervention. As intercessors, we act as mediators, seeking God's forgiveness and grace for others, opening the door for them to receive deliverance that might not come otherwise.

Secondly, identification repentance is a powerful tool within intercessory work. As seen in 2 Chronicles 14:7, repentance goes beyond personal sins and extends to standing in the gap for the sins of others — family, community, or even past generations. When we repent on behalf of others, we break the chains of generational curses and patterns that may be affecting entire bloodlines. This form of repentance acknowledges that we are interconnected, and our prayers can bring freedom not just to ourselves but to those connected to us.

Finally, the effectiveness of intercession is powerfully demonstrated through Daniel's prayer in Daniel 9:1-19. Daniel interceded for his people, confessing their sins and pleading for God's mercy. His heartfelt prayer resulted in divine intervention and restoration. This passage shows how intercession can change the course of history for individuals, families, and even nations. When we pray on behalf of others, we activate the power of God to bring about healing, deliverance, and breakthrough that would not have happened without that prayer. Intercession is not just a prayer — it is a critical act of spiritual warfare that shifts circumstances, and releases God's plans for deliverance.

Instructions: Do not skip them. (Do this with your family before Day 1.)

Altar

Before you begin this book. I encourage you to create an altar. If you don't know what an altar is, it's a place where you go to pray and make a sacrifice (time, money, effort etc.). We're accustomed to going to the altar at church where we give our lives to

Christ or when we need a breakthrough. However, I strongly encourage you to create an altar in your home. This is one spiritual instruction that will help turn the tide of everything around you for good as you engage in these victory prayers.

What can you use to become your altar? You can bless a pillow and put it in the corner of a room or in the place where you're going to pray, and that can be the altar. You can get a small table, and cover it with a cloth and that can become your family altar. If you're single, you can even grab a chair in your home and consecrate the chair as the special place or altar that you'll pray at. Whatever you identify as the altar, use it only for that purpose. You don't have to feel pressured to buy something, though you can if you would like to make that investment.

Why is this important? Because it becomes a place where God answers by fire, and where heaven is open.

In 1 Kings chapter 18, we learn how the prophet Elijah (Elisha's mentor) was challenged by the false prophets of Baal that served under Jezebel, wife of King Ahab and a false teacher. She and King Ahab wanted to, kill, destroy and steal from Elijah, from the true prophets of God, and from the children of God. Behind Jezebel is a vicious spirit that is manipulative and wants to assassinate a person's reputation or assignment.

Jezebel's prophets challenged Elijah to see whose God was the more powerful. They built an altar, and Elijah built an altar. Elijah told them to have their god send fire to the bull sacrifice on the altar to show how powerful he was. He even allowed them to go first. They began to pray to their god for hours and even slashed themselves so they bled ... but *nada* ("nothing" in Spanish), nothing happened. However, when his turn came, Elijah took it to another level. He created a trench around the wood of his altar and flooded it with water, thereby making it practically impossible for it to be lit by fire. Then he prayed to Jehovah God:

"Lord God of Abraham, Isaac, and Israel, let it be known this day that You are God in Israel and I am Your servant, and that I have done all these things at Your word. Hear me, O Lord, hear me, that this people may know that You are the Lord God, and that You have turned their hearts back to You again." (1 Kings 18:36-37 NKJV)

Within seconds, fire came down from heaven and set the sacrifice on the altar on fire. Then the people immediately bowed flat, prostrate on the floor, and said they served the one true God. You serve a God that answers by fire! And your altar will destroy every evil altar that was raised up against you and your bloodline!

Also, think of Jacob in Genesis 28 when he was fleeing the enemy of his past misdeeds, and lay down to rest that night in a deserted place. That night, God gave him a vision of the spiritual reality. He saw the heavens open and there was a ladder that extended from earth to heaven. Angels were descending and ascending right there before him. Then God spoke *"I am the Lord God of Abraham your father and the God of Isaac; the land on which you lie I will give to you and your descendants."*

Shocked he said *"Surely the Lord is in this place, and I did not know it … How awesome is this place! This is none other than the house of God, and this is the gate of heaven!"* (Genesis 28:11-17 NKJV)

Does that remind you of Elisha's servant? How reassuring it is to know that you're not alone! God is with you and He's assigned angels to watch over you. Instead of being oblivious of God's presence, you can now be intentional. Jacob declared that the place was sacred and said "this is the gate of heaven." He called it Bethel, a place of prayer. Your altar is your Bethel. It is a Gate of Heaven!

Don't allow yourself to become freaked out or skeptical about angels ascending and descending from the altar in your home. The scripture says, *"My people are destroyed for lack of knowledge"* (Hosea 4:6). When you are equipped with the knowledge that is going to help you take the offensive versus reacting in defense only, you put yourself in the place of victory.

This is not about encountering an angel; it's about encountering God's presence. You will begin to feel the presence of the Holy Spirit inside of you and the presence of the Lord's angels carrying out those prayers. God appreciates your being intentional about encountering Him. Just like when we're about to watch a movie at the theatre and we put our phones away, so we give our full attention to it, give God your full attention. He said, "Draw nigh to Me and I will draw nigh to you" (James 4:8). When you draw near to Him, you will experience His presence!

The second benefit of the altar is that it defeats demonic altars that the enemy has created. The enemy, satan, uses altars through perversion and puts your family's name and things concerning you on their altars. He and his demons do this to open a portal of destruction that leads to divorce, disease, depression, delay, and death. However, do not be dismayed, because your altar is greater and will destroy their altars immediately!

I strongly encourage you to give an offering on behalf of yourself and your family before beginning. Yes, Jesus paid it all. However, there are some curses and spiritual issues that are only solved through giving. Therefore, after you set up your altar and complete the renouncing prayers (which you will see shortly), find a church or ministry that you can give a monetary offering to. When you do this, do it prayerfully. That means do it with prayer and with faith. Your altar isn't an altar without a sacrifice on it. This is a serious action that is going to kick hell out and tear down strongholds that have been in your family before you even existed. Remember, it didn't start with you, but it stops with you!

If God is leading you to fast during these ten days, ask Him what type of fast He wants you to do. I encourage you to speak with your family about the next ten days. Communicate with your spouse, if you have one, and your children. Perhaps prayer time with your family is not something that you've ever done or considered. Maybe it feels awkward to even bring it up. I encourage you to push past the awkwardness. Maybe you even feel some resistance within yourself because of the ongoing conflict or even years of conflict. Perhaps you and your spouse feel like roommates if you're married, or maybe your children may look at this as something weird to do and may respond with an attitude. Look past that.

There's been an enemy that you can't see that has been in your home. Many times we look at the people around us and we see them as the adversary. However, the adversary has already been there and is stealing from you and your family. Therefore, as you look past the attitudes, direct your focus to defeating the invisible enemy that is actually very real.

This is where your sacrifice of ten minutes begins. A family that prays together, stays together. This is not a cliché. Unity is important. Identify a time that you all will pray each night over the next ten days. Try not to let anything get in the way of that. Be very intentional and strategic just as you are about waking up, dinner time, and showers.

What time will you all pray?

Don't worry if you're unable to meet at the exact second when the time that you have agreed upon comes around. Just do your best to stick to the time over the next ten days. Set an alarm on your phone, so that you follow through.

Renouncing Prayers: Do not skip

You must do the renouncing prayers before you begin Day 1!

Renouncing is important because you are saying that you are coming out of any agreement with the curses, demonic patterns, mindsets and behaviors that have been in the family's bloodline before you were even born. You're saying that you want no part of them by renouncing them. You may notice some statements among the renunciations that may not apply to you. Even if they're something that you do not actively struggle with, I still encourage you to renounce them anyway. You may not know what has been in the bloodline before you, that could try to creep in and impact your kids, or grandkids or future generations. It didn't start with you, but it stops with you!

Now say the following renouncing prayers and, as you renounce, have your family repeat them after you.

Father, we thank You for Your mercy and Your grace. We thank You that Jesus paid the price of sin for all for us, so that we can be free today. We stand in our power and authority of renouncing what we want no part of. As we renounce, we are removing ourselves from any agreement with the kingdom of darkness, and we invite You and Your kingdom to replace what we are no longer a part of. We belong to the body of Christ and we are Your children!

If you are alone, say "I." If you are leading the prayers, say "we."

On behalf of myself and my bloodline, I renounce and reject anything that is not the mindset of Jesus Christ.

I renounce and reject perversion and lust.

I renounce and reject all forms of mental illness.

I renounce and reject all sins of those that came before us – the sins of our ancestors. I repent of those sins as well.

I renounce and reject all witchcraft, psychics, tarot cards, fortune tellers, and occultic practices.

I renounce and reject new ageism.

I renounce and reject trying to understand ourselves through astrology or any source that was not of God.

I renounce and reject fornication, pornography, and masturbation.

I renounce and reject homosexuality.

I renounce and reject incest, child molestation, every form of assault, and rape.

I renounce and reject demonic assignments against marriage that have been against us.

I renounce and reject physical and emotional abuse.

I renounce and reject domestic violence.

I renounce and reject having children out of wedlock.

I renounce and reject adultery.

I renounce and reject divorce.

I renounce and reject abortions and any form of child sacrifice.

I renounce barrenness.

I renounce and reject murder, suicide, and torture.

I renounce self-harm.

I renounce self-mutilation.

I renounce and reject sinning in anger and any form of violence.

I renounce and reject illegal activities.

I renounce being ignorant of the enemy's devices, and rejecting knowledge.

I renounce and reject gluttony.

I renounce emotional eating.

I renounce leaning on my own understanding.

I renounce and reject poverty.

I renounce and reject frivolous spending. I renounce and reject gambling.

I renounce and repent of all debt from before us and that which we've created.

I renounce and reject alcoholism, substance abuse, or any addictions.

I renounce and reject anything that would lead to drunkenness or not having a sober mind.

I renounce and reject cursing and speaking inappropriate words of limitation over ourselves, each other or others.

I renounce and reject lying, gossiping, envy, and jealousy.

I renounce comparing myself with others.

I renounce and reject all forms of idolatry.

I renounce and reject every form of sickness and infirmity.

I repent of all of our sins and the sins of those that came before me. I understand, Father, that it didn't start with me but it stops with me. I ask You to wash me thoroughly and cleanse me and my bloodline from sin. I ask that You forgive our iniquities and remove them. Cleanse and wash us from all transgressions.

Jesus, I ask that You fill me and my bloodline with the light of truth in every part of us, and give us the wisdom to navigate our way moving forward. Create in us a clean heart and renew a right spirit within us. As we are delivered, I thank You that we are deliverers. I thank You that our bloodline is being set free. As You have filled us with Your light, we are the light of the world and we will shine in every dark place. We will use our light to help others come back to You. I thank You and give You the praise! We have overcome because You have already overcome the enemy. The enemy in my home and bloodline is defeated! In Jesus' name, amen!

Final instruction before beginning Day 1

Congratulations! You've taken the next step by completing the renouncing prayers! Tomorrow, we will begin Day 1.

Each chapter has a background on each topic that you are going to declare victory over. It's important for you to read it so that you understand the kind of warfare you are engaging in. Do not be afraid as you are already on the side of victory. After you read over the topic, you will read each prayer point. If you are doing this with your family, you all will be meeting at the time you have agreed on, which will also take place at the altar that you have created, if you have decided to do so.

Once you have completed the prayers, you will see that there is a scripture that you will take just a few minutes to meditate on together.

It is important that you end with this meditation as what has been removed from you NEEDS to be replaced with God's word. Therefore, underneath the scripture is a visualization that you will read while your family's eyes are closed. They need to see themselves in a new light. The word of God says *"The entrance of thy word gives light."* Read the visualization slowly, and even see it in your mind together with your family. You can also access the audio recorded visualization at bonus.stopswithyou.com. These ten minutes that you're sacrificing will break every bondage that has been there for years!

Day 1

Prayers for Healing Mental Illness

There is a mental health crisis that is plaguing millions of people. It does not discriminate. Many children and adults are suffering from anxiety, depression, and mental distress that can be attributed to earlier traumas that they experienced. Some mental illnesses can be caused by a genetic predisposition, meaning that it has been within the family for some time. However, mental illness can also be caused by spiritual issues related to the enemy's desire to oppress you and me.

I remember feeling mentally bombarded and weighed down. I felt my brain was constantly producing thoughts that led me to feel out of control, extreme thoughts that suggested I could harm myself or that I wasn't safe to be around. This made no sense to me because, deep down, I knew that I would never do such a thing, and that I was only interested in being a blessing to others.

One night around 3:00 a.m., I heard a cat meowing. We do not own cats. I have nothing against them, but I don't care for them. I thought it was my one-year old making a weird noise, but I then heard this thought, "I'm trying to show you what's been around you." Instantly, I realized that God was not only speaking to me in that moment, but He opened my spiritual ears to hear what represented a spirit of divination, a deceptive spirit. Its goal is to manipulate your thoughts processes and alter how you see yourself and others. It's witchcraft, which means manipulation.

Ya'll, the devil is wicked. He uses his demons to whisper lies in your ear, so that you internalize them or believe that they are your thoughts. Meanwhile, it is his doing. Beware of his devices!

There are families that have the same or a variety of mental illnesses running through their bloodline. They have been attacking every generation like crazy, to perpetuate anxiety, depression, suicidal ideations, and so on. It didn't start with you, but it stops with you! It's time to stand in your power and authority and pray over yourself and your family to experience freedom. God does not want His people to be in bondage. His word says in 2 Timothy 1: 7: "He did not give us a spirit of fear, but power, love, and a sound mind." Therefore, our baseline emotional and mental well-being should be stable and sound. This is your right as a child of God.

Now is the time to go to the family altar that I encouraged you to set up in the Introduction. If you skipped that part, go back and read the importance of setting up a family altar and praying there together. Altars are not for decoration; they have serious weight in the Spirit, and you will experience a major shift. Did you complete the renouncing prayers before this chapter? If not, begin there.

Now let's get free.

Say "I" if you're by yourself or "we" if with your family.

Prayer:

Father, in Jesus' name, I stand in my authority as a child of God. I acknowledge that you are my Lord and Savior. You became a sin offering and died on the cross so I and my bloodline could be free. You rose again, therefore defeating satan and every infirmity. Father, let the altar that I now have destroy every evil altar against us by Your fire! Father, I pray to receive more power now! I will pray the following prayers confidently, knowing that I will see results.

On behalf of myself, my husband, my children and our respective families:

I bind every mind-binding spirit, and command it to go to the pit in Jesus' name!

You spirit of divination, I remove your power from you, and I bind you! You will not alter my perspective any more or change how I see myself, others, my dreams, or anything concerning me. I command you to go to the pit in Jesus' name!

You spirit of torment, I remove your power from you, and I bind you! You will not torment my mind any longer! I command you to go to the pit in Jesus' name!

Father, by Your stripes, I and my family are healed in Jesus' name!

I cancel and pray against suicidal thoughts in Jesus' name!

Me, my husband, our children, and our families shall live to see the goodness of God in the land of the living!

I pray against and cancel homicidal thoughts and ideations on behalf of my husband, my children and family.

I declare we are peacemakers!

I pray against and cancel anxiety, depression, and all trauma related disorders in Jesus' name!

I pray against and cancel schizophrenia, bipolar disorder, personality disorders, and post-traumatic stress disorder!

I pray against and cancel ADHD and any focus-related disorder as well as any cognitive challenges.

I pray against all other forms of mental illness, and command those illness to be gone. By reason of the blood of Jesus, my bloodline is healed in Jesus' name!

I bind the spirit of slumber (spirit that causes excessive sleep), and command it to go to the bottomless pit in Jesus' name and never return!

I also pray against and cancel restlessness and insomnia now! Father, Your word says in Psalm 127:2, "It is vain for us to rise up early and to sit up late, to eat the bread of sorrow; for You give Your children sleep." I understand there are times where I allowed my thoughts to spiral; however, I come out of agreement with that now. I will cast my cares upon You. I pray You give me sweet sleep in Jesus' name!

Father, Your word says that in this world, we will have tribulation, but we should be of good cheer because You have conquered the world. I pray that You help me to change my perspective of only seeing challenges from my point of view.

I ask that You give me a peace that surpasses my understanding.

As Your word says in Psalm 94:19, "In the multitude of our thoughts, Your comforts delight our soul." I pray for Your comfort when my thoughts are overwhelming!

I cast down every imagination that has exalted itself against Your word. I take every thought captive and will not let those thoughts take me captive any longer! My thoughts shall obey Jesus Christ!

I submit my thoughts to Jesus and I will allow His word to be my mind's filter. If they do not line up with the word, I will immediately cast them down in Jesus' name!

I break any known or unknown agreements with the kingdom of darkness that have impacted me, my husband, my children, and our families' mental health.

I cancel any word curses that any of us or anyone has spoken over me, my husband, our children, and our families.

Father, there are times I have felt hopeless, but I do not want to remain this way. As Your word says in Romans 15:13, YOU ARE the God of hope! Therefore, I pray that You fill me with all joy and peace as I trust in You, so that I may overflow with hope by the power of the Holy Spirit!

I receive a garment of praise (a garment that is literally placed on me in the spiritual realm), and will praise my way out of the spirit of heaviness! (Isaiah 61:3)

I speak blessings and prosperity over my family.

I decree that I, my husband and our children will prosper even as our soul prospers (3 John 2).

Father, there are many times where I've looked outside of You in order to find peace. Forgive me, Father. You promise in Isaiah 26:3 that You will keep me in perfect peace, if I keep my mind on You because I trust in You. Help me to trust You by teaching me Your ways so that I may rely on Your faithfulness.

Father, help me to understand that Your joy operates even during storms. If anything, I need it most during the storms of life. I pray for joy and that You make my joy completely full and overflowing because the joy of the Lord is my strength (Nehemiah 8:10).

Father, give me an undivided heart, so I completely reverence and submit my heart to You. I don't want to operate outside of You, for in You I have peace.

Father, help me to understand my purpose and know that my days here on earth are meaningful.

Father, I acknowledge that there are times that I've allowed the challenges of life, and work schedules to impact my ability to have fun and make exciting memories. Ecclesiastes 9:9 says to enjoy all the days that You have given us. I understand my days are numbered, and I don't want any day wasted. I pray for exciting and fun activities and hobbies so that I may also enjoy my time on earth and with my loved ones.

I declare that it didn't start with me, but it stops with me!

Scripture:

Philippians 4:6-7 NKJV:

Be anxious for nothing, but in everything by prayer and supplication, with thanksgiving, let your requests be made known to God; and the peace of God, which surpasses all understanding, will guard your hearts and minds through Christ Jesus.

Now read the visualization below to your family slowly and ask them to picture what you are saying. This is important as this encourages meditation on God's word, and it helps them to see themselves differently and keep His promises in their heart. If your children are too young to close their eyes and follow along, I encourage you to read it with your spouse or partner, and help them visualize what you are reading. If you are reading it by yourself, visualize it as you read it.

Visualization: Visit bonus.stopswithyou.com to watch and listen to the visualization, and enter the access code 1010.

Philippians 4:6-7 NKJV says:

Be anxious for nothing, but in everything by prayer and supplication, with thanksgiving, let your requests be made known to God; and the peace of God, which surpasses all understanding, will guard your hearts and minds through Christ Jesus.

In this scripture, God is telling us He does not want us to be anxious or afraid about anything and to not allow fear to stifle us or control us. So why do we worry and overwhelm ourselves? This is because of our lack of trust in God. However, God, who is our Father, wants us to know that when we come to Him, for every problem we face, there is a solution. Therefore, the essence and result of your prayer is complete trust that God is working everything out for your good. That trust, leads to the result of peace, which is what the end of that scripture promises us.

Close your eyes, inhale deeply, and settle down comfortably Picture yourself lying in bed. Your mind is filled with thoughts about your interactions that day: your relationships, finances, people's opinions, homework, tests, to-do lists, bills, and what needs to be done tomorrow, etc. However, you decide to release fixating on those things through prayer and faith.

Imagine yourself praying, and see each anxious or negative thought leaving your mind and heart as a red light. Imagine thoughts and fixations about problems you have with others in the form of a red light leaving your mind and heart. Imagine analyzing your interactions with others earlier that day, and also see them as a red light leaving your mind. Imagine thoughts about what people said or their opinions leaving your mind and heart in the form of a red light. Imagine self-criticism leaving your mind and heart in the form of a red light.

Now, see the ceiling open. There's a bright yellow light that comes towards you. This light is God's peace that He sends to fill you up now that you have allowed more room from what you've released. See this light beginning to fill up your mind and heart. Say to yourself, "I have released all the fears and criticisms and receive God's peace." Let this be your meditation.

Consider:

As I am both a therapist and coach, I encourage all to consider receiving counsel/therapy or coaching. Many of us have a troubled mind and relationship with ourselves or we enter into relationships when we are unhealthy and broken due to the trauma and challenges we experienced throughout life.

Now that you've prayed, counsel or coaching can help you implement healthier thoughts and mindsets which will also activate healthier behaviors. Simply put, invest in your mental health and if your children are in need of it, I encourage you to seek it for them as well.

Day 2

Prayers to Recover Your Identity

Millions of people are experiencing an identity crisis. The enemy has attacked identity since the very beginning. When he wants to destroy people, he deceives them. As a result, children and adults are experiencing confusion related to their gender, sexuality, roles, and overall purpose in this world.

When we don't know who we are, we often acquiesce in what is around us or how we feel. However, there is a difference between truth, facts, and feelings. There's only one truth, and in John 14:6, Jesus says, *"I am the way, the truth, and the life: no man cometh unto the Father, but by me."* There are many individuals who have dimmed their light because of people-pleasing, and they are so engulfed in the fear of criticism and rejection that they become detached from themselves.

Many times, we follow after our way or that of others, but know that any way outside of God leads to destruction. I've mentored and counseled many young and older clients who have followed their way and changed aspects of themselves because of the enemy's deceptions. Even after following a trend, pattern, or the feelings of others in their effort to people-please, they still did not experience peace. The by-product of this error was confusion, and emotional pain. I was like that too. I remember dimming my light and going along just to get along.

Now, when we talk about identity, we're talking about your beginning, that is, your foundation. Many of us have the wrong foundation because of how we came into this world or what we experienced in childhood, or what was in the bloodline before us.

There was an evil foundation in my family bloodline, with multiple generational experiences of sexual trauma and rejection. Unless addressed through prayer, counseling, and communication before/with the new generation, these foundations don't just go away.

In speaking with my mom, I found she experienced similar things, and so did my grandmother. These experiences created significant misunderstandings of oneself, leading to not knowing our value, and settling at times (especially within relationships or interactions with people) for less. Not knowing who you truly are (which is, in essence, confusion) can lead to the wrong decisions and connections, resulting in heartbreak after heartbreak. These heart issues (internal) led to constantly altering ourselves (external), which never fixed the problem but only made it worse. This road was a road of destruction where I constantly questioned my worth, and thought it was too difficult to be myself. I was convinced that no one would accept me if they knew me, and therefore made detrimental decisions with my body (external), relationships (external), finances (external) and other areas, because I didn't know my purpose.

However, even in our mistakes, God has extended His grace to us, and there is no decision we can make that can separate us from His love. Our true identity is in Jesus Christ and He has known you since before you can even remember, according to Jeremiah 1:5. Once I understood this, I came back to Him and He accepted me wholeheartedly. This restored me **internally.** That was when I understood who I was, and came to know my purpose. He never leaves us, you see. It's we that leave because we misunderstand (due to leaning into our own understanding or how we see things). This is a device of the enemy. He wants you disconnected from God and connected to chaos, so that you experience cycles of identity theft, crisis, and confusion in your bloodline. Nevertheless, God is our redeemer. His view of you is perfect, and He has the perfect plan and purpose for you and your family.

It's time to use your power and authority, and evict the enemy of chaos, confusion, and identity crisis from your home and your bloodline! These prayers will seal your identity and that of your husband, your children, and your family in Jesus Christ.

Prayer:

Father, I thank You that You have given me the power and authority to declare these prayers, and intercede on behalf of myself, my family and bloodline. You told us to be aware of the enemy's devices so that we are not deceived.

Father on behalf of my husband, our children and our respective families:

I pray that You remove every veil of deception!

Let every evil and ancient foundation on which we have been established be crumbled and removed in Jesus' name. I rebuke the enemy, who has taken advantage of those evil foundations, and command him to leave and never return.

Jesus, You are our foundation and the rock on which we now stand. I pray for divine order and Your perfect will for our lives.

I bind the spirit of deception, and cancel all witchcraft, hexes, vexes, and incantations that have been used against me or my family. I command you spirit of deception to go to the pit in Jesus' name!

No weapon formed against me and my identity shall prosper in Jesus' name and any tongue that rises up against me I condemn (Isaiah 54:17).

I bind the spirit of confusion and chaos, and command it to go to the pit in Jesus' name.

I bind every identity-confusing demon, and command it to go to the pit in Jesus' name.

Father, I've had some negative experiences that have led me to believe that having certain things that are different in me than others is something to feel bad about. I used to feel ashamed, but not any longer. I now come into agreement that I am different because that is how You've made me and I am Your precious child!

When the enemy comes in like a flood, the spirit of the Lord raises up a standard (Isaiah 59:19).I pray that You raise up a standard and establish divine order concerning our identity and purpose in Jesus' name.

Let God arise and let every enemy against me, my husband, children, and family's identity be scattered in Jesus' name.

I renounce all identity issues connected to gender, sexuality, and roles on behalf of my husband, children and family in Jesus' name. I agree with Your word which says You created us male and female and nothing in between (Genesis 1:27).

I pray against any form of spiritual or physical abduction or incarceration against me, my children, and my family in Jesus' name!

Father, close any demonic portals or spiritual doors through which the enemy came in in Jesus' name.

Father, many times I have tried to understand myself through the opinions of others, which negatively impacted how I see myself. I now acknowledge that You are the one who knew me even before I was formed in my mother's womb, and therefore You know me best. Help me to see myself through Your eyes instead of the eyes of others!

Father, there are times where I have dimmed my light because of the fear of people or the fear of rejection. I no longer want to be guided by fear, and operate in a diluted version of myself. Give me the boldness and courage to be all that You have called me to be. As Your word says, "I am the salt and light of the world!" (Matthew 5:13-16)

I come into agreement, that my family of origin was the gateway through which You sent me into this world. I honor them; however, I am who You say I am. No matter what they've experienced even up till now doesn't have to be the end of my story. I declare a new beginning for me and those connected to me!

I only allow the mind of Jesus Christ in me! Father, give me the strength to drive my thoughts towards You.

I decree I will think on things that are true, honest, just, pure, lovely, of good report, virtuous, and praiseworthy (Philippians 4:8).

I decree that I am fearfully and wonderfully made! (Psalm 139:14)

I decree that I have purpose and I am more than a conqueror! (Romans 8:31-39)

Father, I want and need a fresh filling of Your Spirit. Holy Spirit, fill us up and baptize us afresh with Your purifying fire in Jesus' name!

Father, thank You for Your divine intervention. Restore us to Your intended purpose in Jesus' mighty name, amen!

I decree that I, my husband, our children and families will live in accordance with Your design and not the world's design. In Jesus' name.

I declare that it didn't start with me, but it stops with me!

Scripture:

Romans 12:2:

And be not conformed to this world: but be ye transformed by the renewing of your mind, that ye may prove what is that good, and acceptable, and perfect, will of God.

Now read the visualization below to your family slowly and ask them to picture what you are saying. This is important as this encourages meditation on God's word. It helps them to see themselves differently and keep His promises in their heart. If your children are too young to close their eyes and follow along, I encourage you to read it with your spouse or partner and help them picture what you are reading. If you are reading it by yourself, visualize it as you read it.

Visualization: Visit bonus.stopswithyou.com to watch and listen to the visualization, and enter the access code 1010.

Romans 12:2 tells us to not be conformed to this world, but to be transformed by the renewing of our mind so we can demonstrate what is the good, acceptable and perfect will of God. Any time we're conformed to the patterns of the world, it is easy to become lost to the point that we lose our identity, and forget what we are made for. We become versions of ourselves that are not authentic. However, when we conform to God and the image of Jesus Christ, we come to know our truest self.

Close your eyes, take a deep breath and make yourself comfortable. In this visualization, imagine yourself being transported to heaven. You notice its beauty and splendor. You see that the streets are paved with gold and there is a bright light everywhere you look. The bright light is radiating from God Himself as He shines everywhere because He's omnipresent. You notice this all-pervasive sense of peace and belonging. This is because you are a child of God and your identity is in Him.

On your head is a crown, and on your body is a white robe with other royal colors. The feelings of fear and confusion about who you are no longer exist because now you know where you came from and who you belong to. Examine your clothes and your crown. You begin to hear God speaking to you. He tells you that you were born for a purpose and He is always with you.

Now see yourself leaving heaven and being brought back to earth. You have returned with the confidence that leads you to focus on conforming to the image of Jesus Christ instead of the patterns in the world. You are a leader and are chosen to do great and mighty things that will help your generation! Let this be your meditation.

Consider:

Grab some paper and pens for you and your family. Have you and your family write down seven "I am" statements. For example: "I am a female child of God, made in His image." Assist younger children as needed. These "I am" statements speak to who you are because you now have clarity about whose you are (a child of God!). You can share your I am statements with each other after you all have finished them. I also encourage you to keep those statements close to you. You can even have your children place theirs on their wall and say them daily!

Just as the enemy clocks in daily to seek opportunities to deceive, discourage, and deplete us, we all need to affirm DAILY who we are in Christ!

Day 3

Prayers to Defeat Perversion and Lust

In the same way the enemy attacks identity, he likes to create the wrong version of everything. Our Father is a creator but the enemy is a copycat. He does not want you to live a life that is holy and acceptable to God. Yes, we will make mistakes; however, the enemy wants your mistakes to derail you.

Thank God, we are covered by His grace and protection. Adults who become lustful were many times victims of someone else's lust in their childhood or young adult years. This is the assignment of the spirit of lust and the spirit of perversion. Many times, evil spirits work together. I've heard many cases of individuals being introduced to pornography or inappropriate conversations for their age during their childhood years. They then become obsessed or infatuated with these things because the perversion entices them and causes a chemical release in their brain associated with pleasure. However, after engaging in these activities many times, they feel disgusted and guilty. These activities always leave them lacking and wanting more because there are voids in the individual that are being filled in the wrong way.

As a result of this, I've seen many marriages end in divorce because of the unrealistic expectations attached to sexual intimacy. The practice of pornography or lustful thinking to put pressure on sex to be a reenactment of pornographic scenes results in many marriage beds becoming defiled. Lust is also behind fornication and promiscuity. There is a battle in the mind. Often, they we overwhelmed by intrusive and inappropriate thoughts that cause us to feel a loss of control over their thoughts and emotions. This has been the enemy's strategy from the very beginning.

To counter this, be aware AND honest. Don't let what is a weakness turn into full-blown wickedness because you're not truly honest with yourself about where you are. Perhaps this doesn't apply to you, but may apply to someone in your family line. Nevertheless, you can take back control no matter how long you had certain thought patterns or habitual behaviors or how long it's been in the bloodline. We must pray against the enemy's plot to pervert us, and our families. No matter what evil spirits are working together against you and your family, you can stand together and defeat their assignment. These issues did not start with you, but they stop with you.

Prayer:

Father, I thank You that You have given us power and authority to stand in the gap for our children and our families. I pray, knowing that these prayers will shift any issue concerning me, my husband, children and our families.

Father on behalf of my husband, our children and our families:

I renounce all forms of sexual immorality including child molestation, sexual assault and rape, fornication, pornography, masturbation, promiscuity, bestiality, and all other forms of perverted sexuality in Jesus' name.

I bind the spirit of perversion that creates the wrong version of things in our bloodline, minds and relationships, and command it to go to the pit in Jesus' name.

I bind every unclean spirit that leads to unclean acts, and command it to go to the pit in Jesus' name.

I bind the spirit of confusion around sexual matters, and command it to go to the pit in Jesus' name.

I bind the spirit of *cozbi* (a lustful spirit), and command it to go to the pit in Jesus' name.

I bind the seducing spirits that whisper lies to lead me into temptation. and command them to go to the pit in Jesus' name.

I bind the spirit of lasciviousness (offensive sexual behavior), and command it to go to the pit in Jesus' name.

I bind the spirits of Delilah and Jezebel (seducing and manipulative spirits), and command them to go to the pit in Jesus' name.

I bind the spirit of lust, and command it to go to the pit in Jesus' name.

I divorce any spirit wife or spirit husband that has slept with me in my dreams. I remove any ring you've placed on my finger in the spiritual realm. I command all you spirits to go to the pit in Jesus' name, and everything associated with what you've done to be consumed by fire in Jesus' name!

I cancel the assignment of the enemy to plant seeds of perversion. I curse any seed of perversion that has been planted to the root, and I uproot it now in Jesus' name.

Father, cut off any ungodly soul ties from past or current relationships.

Father, I do not understand all of my errors, and I ask You to cleanse me and my bloodline from secret faults. Remove all iniquity from me! Keep me away from presumptuous sins, and do not allow those sins to have dominion over me! As a result, I shall be upright and I shall be innocent of great transgression! (Psalm 19:12-14).

Father, You are the Lord, the God of all flesh; nothing is too hard for You! I now understand that I am not too much for You to handle, and Your grace and love cover and purify me. Father, deliver me and my bloodline from our flesh!

I pray against any unhealthy relationships that we have with ourselves and various parts of our body.

I declare that we are disciplined and have a healthy relationship with our bodies as our bodies are the temple of the Holy Spirit.

I pray that You bless our children to have a healthy relationship with their bodies as they experience puberty and age.

I speak healing and restoration over our bloodline right now.

I pray against any indecent exposure, and cancel any assignment of the enemy to expose me, my spouse, or my children to anything perverse whether that be through conversations, literature, the internet, and any form of media.

I pray that the wrong relationships be removed from any of us, and that we do not entertain what is inappropriate.

Father, I ask that You restore any fragmented parts of our souls as a result of trauma in Jesus' name.

Father, I pray against any physiological and mental health issues that came as a result of sexual trauma, and I pray for healing in Jesus' name, amen.

Father, I pray against inappropriate sexual fantasies and inappropriate intrusive thoughts in Jesus' name.

According to Proverbs 6:16-19: "There are six things the Lord hates, seven that are an abomination to Him: haughty eyes, a lying tongue, hands that shed innocent blood, a heart that devises wicked schemes, feet that are quick to rush into evil, a false witness who pours out lies and a person who stirs up conflict in the community." I decree that what is an abomination to God is an abomination to me!

I pray against and cancel any assignment of human sex trafficking.

Father, I ask that You restore me, my husband, our children and our families' heart, and help us to guard it appropriately so that we do not allow perverse thoughts to enter.

Father, I pray that You soften any stubborn or hardened parts of our hearts as a result of trauma or repetitive behaviors that have caused us to become emotionally unstable or numb.

I pray for a healthy view of sex and sexual intimacy in the context of marriage.

Father, I ask that Your word become activated in me, my husband, our children and our families that we may not sin against You.

Create in us a clean heart, and renew a right spirit within us.

Thank You that Your grace covers a multitude of sins and Your perfect love purifies us.

Father, may we get to know Your perfect love for us more than ever.

Father, give me the grace to accept the truth and the gift of freedom, that You've given me. I will no longer believe I am in bondage, but will walk in freedom. Whoever the Son sets free is free indeed and I am free of lust and perversion!

Holy Spirit, fill every void and emptiness on the inside of us so that we may be full of You instead of the pleasures of this world or the flesh.

Father, I pray for strength in every weakened place within me and my family so that we may be fortified.

Purge and purify our hearts so that we can see You!

I will no longer see myself as unclean. I am pure because You have purified me!

Father, thank You for answering our prayers!

I declare that it didn't start with me, but it stops with me!

Scripture:

Psalm 51:6 NKJV:

Behold, You desire truth in the inward parts, And in the hidden part You will make me to know wisdom.

Visualization: Visit bonus.stopswithyou.com to watch and listen to the visualization, and enter the access code 1010.

Psalm 51:6 says, "Lord, we desire truth in our inward parts and wisdom in our hidden parts." David was a man who committed adultery and murder because he had lust in his heart. When he repented, he asked God to allow truth as well as wisdom to come into his inward parts. He asked for truth because lust and perversion are connected to lies that cause us to be impulsive and seek temporary pleasures. He asked God for wisdom so he would operate according to God's instruction, instead of his impulsivity.

When we come to know the truth, it will set us free. Close your eyes, breathe deeply and make yourself comfortable. Imagine yourself in a place where there isn't light. It's dark, but you now know to turn to God, so His light may shine on you and in you. You've asked God to help you overcome any form of perversion and lustful thinking. You are now open to receiving His light and that activates you to think purely and operate in the power that He has given you.

You then feel God's love surround you. He says, "My child, I have brought you out of darkness into My marvelous light."

Begin to see yourself once in darkness, but God stretching His mighty loving hand, removing you from darkness and placing you in complete bright light. See His white light surround you. This is the light of God which is filled with His love and truth. It begins to enter you. See it entering you and every body part that you may have had an unhealthy relationship with. See it going to every inward place so that no darkness can remain. See the darkness leave. You begin to hear God say, "I love you, my precious and pure child. Your body is the temple of the Holy Spirit. You are no longer a slave to sin but you are now free as My light of truth and love is in you. As you focus on Me, I will continue to fill you and you will remain free." Take a deep breath and open your eyes. Let this be your meditation.

Consider:

I strongly encourage you to look at your children's electronics whether that be a chromebook, tablet, regular laptop or phone if they are under the age of eighteen. Do this at least every three months or by the prompting of the Holy Spirit. You may think, "Not my child"; however, even pastor's children struggle. You may be surprised at what your children may look at. I encourage you to put safeguards to discourage them from visiting inappropriate websites.

I also encourage you to have healthy conversations with your children about their bodies, setting healthy boundaries, and knowing God's design for sex and marriage. You may even be surprised at how early these conversations are already happening and how early the exposure to pornography can be. One of my children told me about conversations she was having in the 3rd and 4th grade, which is elementary school! I have also heard of cases as early as elementary school where magazines or websites are visited and shared amongst peers. The enemy does not care how cute your kids are: he is intent on destroying them as early as possible. **Do not be naïve. Be non-negotiable**. Yes, be non-negotiable about your kids' spiritual health, emotional health, and mental health.

If you are struggling with pornography, I encourage you to download software onto your computer, phone, and other electronics that can help keep you accountable and reinvent healthy images and thoughts in your mind. This is only the beginning of freedom as healing and wholeness is a process. The enemy has left strongholds in your mind that need to be broken and pulled down daily by renewing your mind. You can also consider therapy if needed. Don't allow shame to keep you from getting help, as we all need help. You can overcome. You overcoming ensures that your children overcome as well!

Day 4

Prayers for Healthy Emotional Well-Being

I've worked with many individuals who experience emotional highs and lows or emotional instability. One moment they are content, the next they are irritable, and then they're sad. Some have difficulty seeing what is right because everything feels wrong.

Many of us are not taught emotional intelligence or how to control our emotions. We are told to just get over it or be quiet. A few spirits behind this are the spirits of fear, anger, and rejection (emotional neglect). Perhaps we were invalidated or dismissed growing up, so we then become adults who compartmentalize our feelings. Compartmentalization is a defense mechanism in which conflicting thoughts and feelings are kept separated or isolated from each other in the mind. Or we may invalidate the feelings of others by dismissing or rejecting their thoughts, feelings, or behaviors.

The enemy likes to go through doors that are open. Doors in our hearts become open when there are unresolved issues stemming from painful experiences. I've heard one person say, "Pain that is not transformed is transmitted, and hurt people will hurt people."

Sometimes we even become defensive because we've experienced so much hurt throughout the years which can lead to issues with pride. We then have the need to be right. Some of us are told that we're too sensitive or that we are complaining instead of learning how to calm ourselves down and communicate our needs in a healthy way. I remember seeing physical conflict between my parents in my childhood (which was also an evil foundation discussed earlier). This was traumatic and created anxiety within me. That along with other experiences led me to compartmentalize my feelings, afraid to communicate my needs due to fear of some sort of retaliation or rejection. This was an open door that the enemy stepped in and took advantage of.

It was no coincidence that there was domestic violence in my parents' relationship. They were hurt people hurting each other because they did not have healthy conflict resolution or communication skills. It didn't start with them. Their parents experienced similar issues.

Therefore, emotional instability can be attributed to earlier experiences, challenges, or traumas that are passed down. Familiar spirits, which are spirits that follow a family's bloodline, will come generation after generation to ensure the same cycles happen and repeat.

What does your inner voice sound like? If you were raised in a home where you were constantly criticized and not taught to appreciate yourself, this can lead to emotional hostility within yourself where you are constantly criticizing yourself. One coach put it this way: self-criticism is self-hatred. That may sound extreme; however, begin to think about how you talk to yourself. If some of you were to talk to others the way you talk to yourself, conflict could arise.

In fact, many of us become our own worst enemies because of how hostile we are on the inside towards ourselves. This is derived from past hurts or the semblance of humility by being self-critical, but it's not the same thing. True humility is not being prideful or boasting while acknowledging (appreciating) your assets (intrinsic gifts/materials, etc.) with the desire to continue to grow. Whatever our inner tendencies, it is now our responsibility to heal and experience wholeness, without the need for someone to apologize for hurting you. Perhaps you do not like what I just said and you demand your apology. Well, if you make yourself wait for an apology, what you are doing is delaying your peace.

Peace is a decision that you have to give yourself permission to experience. This begins with forgiving the people who hurt you and forgiving yourself. Additionally, you must ask God for wisdom on how to move forward if you are still connected to those people, or if you need to disconnect from those people and implement healthy boundaries.

God wants us to be healed so that we are mentally and emotionally healthy. Our freedom is our children's freedom. It's time for those generational patterns of emotional instability to cease, and for us and our children to be wise and to learn how to be emotionally intelligent. We begin healing by receiving God's perfect love for us and truly loving ourselves. Many times too, we place high expectations on people and end up disappointed because they are not perfect. But God is the only one that is perfect and who will not disappoint you. He knows your needs and wants and will give them to you accordingly. He wants to have a relationship with you and your family. Receiving His love enables you to love yourself. It is from loving yourself that you can love others, and operate from a place of calmness and compassion.

Prayer:

Father, I thank You that You have given us power and authority to stand in the gap for our children and our families. I pray, knowing that these prayers will shift any issue concerning me, my husband, our children and our families.

Father, there are hurts and disappointments that I've experienced in my childhood and adult relationships. There were times where I felt rejected and criticized by others, and it led me to devalue myself or harbor resentment. This resentment has led to emotional instability. This has impacted not only me, but those connected to me. I want to forgive. I now recognize that forgiveness is not a feeling but a decision that will allow healing to take place. I forgive those who have hurt me and disappointed me. I also forgive myself.

I renounce any thoughts or ideas that suggest that acting out of anger or sadness "is who I am." I now realize that You intend for me and those connected to me to be mentally and emotionally stable!

On behalf of my husband, my children, and the families we were born into:

I bind the spirit of anger, and command it to go to the pit in Jesus' name.

I declare that we can be angry, but not sin because we do not hold on to anger (Ephesians 4:26-27).

I bind the spirit of pride, and command it to go to the pit in Jesus' name.

Father God, hook the spirit of Leviathan (serpent of pride discussed in the book of Job), and cut off its head in Jesus' name!

I bind every manipulative spirit, and command it to go to the pit in Jesus' name.

I bind the spirit of fear, and command it to go to the pit in Jesus' name.

I decree that we shall let go of past resentment.

I pray for control over our emotions and for emotional stability.

Father, help us to make peace with the past, and peace with the actions of our parents or those who raised us.

Father, restore our souls so that we can prosper (3 John 2).

Father, I pray that You lead us to resources so that we can all learn to control our emotions and communicate our needs in a healthy way.

You have not given us a spirit of fear, but power love, and a sound mind (2 Timothy 2:7).

Father, I allowed anxious thoughts to alter my way of thinking. I formed patterns of imagining the worst-case scenarios, but it has only plagued my mind and caused emotional instability. I release any need I've created in myself to be anxious as a result of past traumas.

Father, I release the need to be defensive or to be right, which has caused arguments and division in my relationships.

I allow myself the grace to listen and speak in wisdom and not impulsively, for I have to answer for every idle or negative word spoken against myself or others on Judgment day (Matthew 12:36). I pray for wisdom right now and thank You for it!

Father, I pray against holding grudges, vindictive behavior, and selfish behaviors.

Father, teach us how to guard our heart for out of it flows the issues of life (Proverbs 4:23).

Father, allow peace that surpasses our understanding to come into our hearts (Philippians 4:7).

I release every mindset that is creating sabotage within us and affecting our emotions right now in Jesus' name.

Father, give us wisdom on how to better handle our emotions.

I declare that it didn't start with me, but it stops with me!

Scripture:

Proverbs 16:32:

He that is slow to anger is better than the mighty, and he that ruleth his spirit than he that taketh a city.

Visualization: Visit bonus.stopswithyou.com to watch and listen to the visualization, and enter the access code 1010.

Proverbs 16:32 says *"He that is slow to anger is better than the mighty, and he that ruleth his spirit than he that taketh a city."* This scripture reveals that not only is it powerful for you to have control over your emotions, but a person that has control over their emotions is actually stronger than an army taking over a city.

Being impulsive or allowing anger to rule us is dangerous and can lead to destruction. However, controlling your emotions will empower you to overcome anything that comes your way.

The enemy is not powerful but is strategic and wants to provoke you and push your buttons. Do you know the saying, "He that angers you controls you?" It's time for you to take back control. Begin to imagine a recent trigger that involved a person. Perhaps in this scenario, you did not respond with calmness and healthy communication. Reflect on your response. Many times, we feel vindicated or justified in our response, not realizing that it only creates more issues, isolation and disconnection.

1 Corinthians 13:4-9 NIV says:

Love is patient, love is kind. It does not envy, it does not boast, it is not proud. It does not dishonor others, it is not self-seeking, it is not easily angered, it keeps no record of wrongs. Love does not delight in evil but rejoices with the truth. It always protects, always trusts, always hopes, always perseveres. Love never fails. But where there are prophecies, they will cease; where there are tongues, they will be stilled; where there is knowledge, it will pass away.

Love is the greatest.

God is love, and God is in you. Therefore, you must operate from the understanding that your entire being is love, because God dwells in you. It's not about you continuing to react in a certain way because you think you've always been that way or because it has been a habit. No, it's about you dying to who you thought you were, and operating from a new state of being because of the Divine being (who is our Creator) is inside of you. Deciding to be calm is not a weakness, and your calmness is not contingent upon others being calm. You will not be controlled by anybody else's emotions any longer.

Now knowing what you know, it's time to redo this scenario. Close your eyes, take a deep breath and settle in a comfortable position. See yourself remaining calm, regardless of what the person is doing or what is happening. Take three deep breaths right now. Deep breath one. Deep breath two. Deep breath three.

Genuinely say in your heart: "I choose to remain calm. I choose to receive the peace of God so I can see this clearly. I am love. I am patient. I am kind. I am not envious or prideful. I choose not to dishonor or be easily angered. I no longer keep a record of wrongs. I do not delight in evil but I rejoice with the truth. I am protective, trusting and hopeful in God who helps me to persevere through every situation. Vengeance is His, and my allowing Him to vindicate me allows me to always be victorious. Now see how controlling your emotions has changed the atmosphere.

Consider:

"Knowledge without implementation is just a rumor" is one of my favorite quotes. Try implementing what you have now seen yourself do into a scenario this week.

When you do, come back and write about that outcome.

What was the scenario? Who was involved? How did you respond? How is this different from previous scenarios?

Day 5

Prayers to Defeat Addiction

Addiction is dependence on a particular substance that individuals develop when they try to escape mental and emotional anguish. I've spoken with many individuals who became addicted to substances such as alcohol, marijuana, cocaine, pornography, food and even social media. The spirits behind addiction are spirits of shame, perversion, lust, rejection, an addictive spirit, and familiar spirits. Addiction then becomes a disease because there is *dis-ease* or a lack of peace. They are looking for reprieve or pleasure to replace the pain that they're in. I truly believe that no one wakes up and says I want to be an addict.

Many Christians and people in general also have secret addictions due to generational trauma that they have not healed from. These sources will run dry and will never fill the void you may be experiencing and give you the peace you truly desire. There are also others who have an addictive personality, that is, once they try one of these substances, they usually become hooked. The enemy is always looking for an open door, and when it seems the addiction was completely random and unexpected of the person, it's likely that it didn't start with him. Perhaps you didn't know that family members in the bloodline had addictive personalities or struggled with addiction. Unless this issue is addressed through prayer, relationship with God, and counsel, this pattern can continue to be passed down.

I remember how I once formed an unhealthy relationship with wine. I had to give it up because I was using it as a crutch. I began to notice a pattern. I'd be stressed out and that was what I would pick up. My mother, who had moved in with us to help with our children, began to notice this and was gravely concerned. However, I would dismiss her concern, because I said "Jesus made wine and turned the water into wine, hallelujah!" Well, just because He made it, doesn't mean He drank it to excess and was reliant on it for His moods!

I later learned that within my family, there were many alcoholics and the death of one of my aunts was attributed to alcoholism. This was why my mother was so concerned. In hindsight, I appreciate her sharing this information with me. When there has been something in the bloodline, it is important to warn your children, not out of a place of fear but out of a place of wisdom.

So, we see addictions are unhealthy relationships and reliance on something to allay our moods. Jesus prioritized His **relationship** with His Father, making God the Father His one true source of dependence. That made Him prioritize sobriety and purity.

We want those generational issues to stop with this generation. Never allow shame to keep information that can be beneficial when shared at an appropriate time. This is supported by the scripture, *"Train up your child in the way they should go so when they're older they will not depart from it"* (Proverbs 22:6). How do we train our new generation? Teach them how to develop their own relationship with God. Having this family pray during family altar time is teaching them how to come together in unity and pray. Meditating on scripture is helping them to have a healthy flow of God's thoughts in their mind. Having discussions with them about your upbringing in a healthy way and giving them advice is training them up. Putting them in activities that encourage their gifts and their self-esteem is also training them and creating a trajectory of success.

The main lesson is that God is the true and only source that will fill every void, and give us the peace that the world or any substance cannot.

Prayer:

Father, thank You for giving us power and authority to stand in the gap for our children and families. I pray, knowing that these prayers will shift any issue concerning me, my husband, my children and the families we were born into.

Father, You know everything concerning us and all of the issues and trauma that led to choosing other sources leading to addictions. Even if my household is not struggling with any addictions, we want to ensure that the root of them is cut off, and we pray against any assignment of the enemy against us.

Father, we pray that this revelation defeats any excuses or rationalizing of issues, so we can receive the help that we need, and heal.

On behalf of my husband, my children, and the families we were born into:

Spirit of shame, I divorce you. I am not my past. I am not my past mistakes. I disconnect myself from you. You will not dictate my thoughts or actions any longer. I evict you now. I bind you, and I command you to go to the pit in Jesus' name!

I bind any familiar spirit that has been following my family bloodline to trap us in a cycle of addiction. I command that spirit to go to the pit in Jesus' name!

I bind the spirit of rejection and confusion that can lead to self-rejection and disconnection from you and dependence on alcohol or drugs. I command it to go to the pit in Jesus' name!

I bind the spirit of addiction to alcohol and any substance, and command it to go to the pit in Jesus' name.

I pray against any spirit behind lies and sabotage. I and those connected me allow only the Holy Spirit to lead us into all truth! It is the truth that sets us free!

Father, there is an opioid crisis. Many have become addicted as a result of surgeries, pain management or other causes. I pray that I or anyone connected to me do not fall into this trap or cycle. If anyone connected to me has fallen into this, let it be broken now in Jesus' name! I command us to be loosed from it now in Jesus' name!

I, my husband, children, nieces, and nephews will not give in to peer pressure to use marijuana in various forms, alcohol, vapes, or any substance sought to fulfill the desires of the flesh or to alter our state of mind.

I break off all drug addictions, and I pray that You loose us from any bondage that we're in.

Father, break any other type of addiction off of us and our bloodline now in the mighty name of Jesus.

Father, I understand that we will experience trials and tribulations on this earth, but You told us to be of good cheer because You have overcome the world. Therefore, help us to heal and develop a perspective in which we see ourselves as overcomers and more than conquerors instead of being overcome by our circumstances.

As You deliver us, I pray that You increase our resistance to all temptation and I thank You that You always provide a way of escape (1 Corinthians 10:13).

I pray that any past open doors or gates to drug use, be shut now in Jesus' name!

Father, give us strength as we experience deliverance.

Your strength is perfect in our weaknesses. I do not have to fix myself before coming to You, as You are the one who cleanses us from all diseases and hurts. You are a father to the fatherless and a mother to the motherless. I thank You that You are everything that we need.

Holy Spirit, help us to be surrendered to You so we do not miss out on an encounter with You, which is our daily portion.

Father, there are times that I allowed shame to keep me from getting support. However, Your word says there is no condemnation to those in Christ Jesus, who walk not after the flesh but after the spirit (Romans 8:1-2). I thank You that I am not condemned. I declare that I will not allow shame to stop me from getting any help that I need such as counseling, coaching or support groups.

Father, You declare that Your sheep hear Your voice and a stranger's voice we will not follow (John 10:4-5). I will not follow a stranger's voice that is telling us to continue with any addiction.

Father, I ask that You change our appetite from the things of the world, to You.

I pray that You make every crooked way straight within us.

Father, You said those that hunger and thirst after righteousness shall be filled. I no longer want to be filled with the things of this world but I want a supernatural filling. Jesus, we invite You into our heart. We pray that You put us in right standing with You, and I ask that You fill us up right now.

I cast my cares upon You because You care for us.

Father, Your word talks about the importance of being sober-minded so that we are aware of the enemy's devices. I want my mind to be clear and vigilant, so I am not devoured by the devil! I pray for a renewed mind. Cleanse my conscience and subconscious mind. Help me to remove thought patterns that are not of You, and replace them with patterns of the mind of Christ.

Father, I acknowledge that at times I have been naïve to what is happening around me spiritually. I am spirit, soul and body. I no longer want to just be aware of what is happening physically, but also of what's happening spiritually. Holy Spirit, teach me to see beyond what I can see in the natural. Open my spiritual eyes, as You did with Saul who You turned into Paul.

I declare that we will put our trust in You and depend on You because You are our source.

I declare that I am bought with a price and my body is the temple of the Holy Spirit.

Father, we thank You that You want to have a relationship with us. We thank You that we are not orphans, forgotten or cast aside. We thank You that we are Your children.

Father, we thank You that You literally gave up Your life for us because You love us so much. Help us to understand the depths of Your love This by itself will break off every addiction as we acknowledge that truly You are our one true source.

I declare that it didn't start with me, but it stops with me!

Scriptures:

Psalm 27:10:
When my father and my mother forsake me, then the Lord will take me up.

Psalm 139:8-10:
If I ascend up into heaven, thou art there: if I make my bed in hell, behold, thou art there. If I take the wings of the morning, and dwell in the uttermost parts of the sea; Even there shall thy hand lead me, and thy right hand shall hold me.

Visualization: Visit bonus.stopswithyou.com to watch and listen to the visualization, and enter the access code 1010.

Many of us experience disappointments in our relationships. You may have experienced disappointments growing up with your parents, family members, friends, or even now with spouses, at work, church, and other places. Nevertheless, the Father wants us to know that He will never leave us. We know that no one but He is perfect, but even in the scripture, Psalm 27:10, He is saying that our parents have limited capacity. Many times, we expected more from them than they were able to give. Many times too, we expect more from people than they are able to give. We become disappointed, and our pain is valid; however, God takes us and heals us. He even divinely connects us with new individuals that will aid in our healing journey. We don't have to go and isolate ourselves or look to things that will only provide temporary relief but will ultimately destroy us.

Psalms 139:8-10 says:

If I ascend up into heaven, thou art there: if I make my bed in hell, behold, thou art there. If I take the wings of the morning, and dwell in the uttermost parts of the sea; Even there shall thy hand lead me, and thy right hand shall hold me.

God is showing us He is everywhere, and you are not too much for Him to handle. Close your eyes, take a deep breath and get yourself comfortable. Imagine there is a chain on you, connecting you to that addiction. Now you've decided to lean on God, who commands the chain to fall off. See yourself walking away from the addiction. Now begin to see yourself like a child in His arms. His light is so bright and is shining all around you. None of those dark situations from the past are weighing you down any longer. You are feeling lighter, even as He is lifting you in His arms. In His arms, you are protected. As you are near Him, you feel His heartbeat and the warmth of His love embracing you. You may even begin to feel His presence right now surrounding you. In His presence, there is fullness of joy and freedom. Soak up His light and watch it as it enters you. Enjoy His presence, which will remain with you everywhere you go. Let this be your meditation.

Consider:

If applicable, consider writing down the addictions that you are now deciding to part with. This is like making a promise to yourself and to those connected to you. You can write "I'm deciding to part ways with x, y, and z." Sign at the bottom of it. As you make this decision and identify it, consider receiving support, such as counseling, coaching, or a support group. Receiving support is something we have to give ourselves permission to receive. Don't allow shame to keep you isolated. Many of us need accountability and support, so we can ensure that we are taking steps in our healing process.

Day 6

Prayers for Breaking Poverty and for Financial Prosperity

The financial blueprint that we currently have is the one that was handed to us or the one that we grew up around. If your parents took out loans, it's likely that you may be taking out loans. If your parents did not save money and quickly spent it, it's likely that you will do the same.

I remember developing the same pattern as my parents and asking God to change things for me financially. He began to give me witty ideas to produce wealth. I began to utilize my gifts and write books, open businesses, and invest in coaching so that I could be successful.

Conversely, if your parents saved money and paid off their debts, it is likely that you will manage your finances well. We watch, we listen, and we repeat. They're also financial issues that can be related to spiritual issues. I've heard of many cases where some debt was owed, and a curse was spoken over the family by the person who wanted their money back. Therefore, even generations after, the persons who owed money were suffering financially or were striving to make progress in life.

Nevertheless, God who is rich in mercy is the one that paid it all for our prosperity. Not only does He give us the power to make wealth, He can cancel our debts in the spirit realm. For this to work we must follow God's laws in regarding to sowing and reaping. I do encourage you to pay your tithes, which is just 10% of your increase, and to give offerings. This is an act of obedience that can produce a discipline that yields good stewardship. God does not need our money; remember that it all belongs to

Him. However, when we tithe, He says He will rebuke the devourer for our sake. Who is the devourer? The devourer is an evil spirit that eats people's finances. Also, every time you give an offering, do it intentionally. Tell God why you're doing it like you did in the beginning of this prayer journey.

Job gave an offering every day on behalf of his children because he knew their vulnerabilities. His offering was like an insurance policy of "just in case they sinned today." He also wanted God to give them an undivided heart, so they could always reverence God. Imagine the great extent that he went to just to make sure his children were covered. How much more should we do than we're currently doing to make sure our children are covered daily! He wanted to make sure they made heaven! I've given offerings specifically on behalf of my children. I've also given seed offerings on behalf of other enterprises that I wanted God to bless. I put seed in good soil (a church/ministry), so I could reap a harvest later.

This was an act of faith, saying, "God I'm believing for a harvest in this area so I'm going to plant a seed for this project or enterprise Not only did I receive increase, but during times of economic drought, I would receive checks from the previous year that didn't make sense. God moved supernaturally to ensure I was sustained. God sees the sacrifice and honors it. There are some patterns and curses that are broken with prayer, and there are some that are broken with an offering, so this is very important. God does not want us to lack, but to be prosperous in every area of our life!

Prayer:

Father, thank You for giving us power and authority to stand in the gap for our children and families. I pray, knowing that these prayers will shift any issue concerning me, my husband, our children and our families.

On behalf of my husband, my children, and family of origin:

Father, forgive us for the times that we did not tithe or give an offering when You were leading us to.

Father, You say in Proverbs 3:9 to honor You with our possessions and with the first fruits of all our increase, so our barns will be filled with plenty and our vats will overflow. Father, there are times where I did not honor You with my first fruits and, out of desperation, gave You my leftovers. However, I am now understanding that giving my first fruits is putting my trust in You for my supply and acknowledging that it is You who sustains me.

Father, You said that You give seed to the sower. Thank You for seeds that You have given us so that we may sow and reap a harvest. Lead us to the ministries with good soil, to tithe and sow into.

Father, rebuke the Devourer for our sake.

I bind any spirit that is connected to financial issues, and I command it to go to the pit and never return in Jesus' name.

I command any spirit that is holding on to and stealing our wealth to loose it now in Jesus' name!

I speak to every financial crisis in my bloodline: you shall know wealth, in Jesus' name!

Father, I pray for seven-fold restitution in Jesus' name! (Proverbs 6L30-31)

Father, I thank You that You became poor so that we wouldn't have to be. Thank You that it is not meant for us to live in poverty and be impacted by failures in the world's economy.

According to Deuteronomy 8:18, You have given us the power to make wealth. Father, give us ideas including businesses that we have forgotten about that we may utilize what You have given us to make wealth.

Father, we ask that every spiritual debt be completely wiped away, even debt that came from our parents before us.

I decree that we will have the best credit scores.

Father, forgive me for frivolous spending and not having healthy financial boundaries. There are times I may have also criticized others for how they used money, but I have not considered my own use of money.

I decree that we will not be frivolous in our spending but we will be good stewards over everything that You have already predestined for us to have.

If I need to invest in financial literacy for financial classes, I will do it so that I do not repeat the same mistakes of those before us.

Father, I ask that You shift our mindsets from financial insecurity, food insecurity and poverty to a mindset that is kingdom and abundance centered.

I allow the mind of Jesus Christ to be inside of me!

I decree that I believe in the kingdom of God's economy over the world economy. I will experience abundance and multiplicity no matter what the world is going through.

I decree that our businesses shall always prosper.

I decree that we are lenders and not borrowers.

I decree that we will make our payments on time and before time. We will no longer be late as it is a blessing to pay our bills and pay off all of our debts.

I decree that we will no longer live from paycheck to paycheck.

I decree that You have put within us ideas so that we can and will have up multiple streams of income.

I decree that we will leave an inheritance for our children's children.

I decree that everything concerning us shall be full and overflowing.

Father, bless us and our children with grants and scholarships.

I decree that we will not serve Mammon, but we will only serve You Father. Money will serve us and what we are doing for the kingdom of God.

I decree that money will never become an idol and You are always first. As You increase us, we will not forget where we came from and what You have done for us.

Father, we pray that our household makes financial decisions that are not impulsive. Instead, we will acknowledge You in all our ways and allow You to direct our path. We will not allow finances to divide us and we will have healthy conversations about finance.

Father, I thank You so much for the ability and the power to create wealth. May You get the glory from everything that we do in the mighty name of Jesus!

I declare that it didn't start with me, but it stops with me!

Scripture:

Deuteronomy 8:18:

But thou shalt remember the LORD thy God: for it is he that giveth thee power to get wealth, that he may establish his covenant which he sware unto thy fathers, as it is this day.

Visualization: Visit bonus.stopswithyou.com to watch and listen to the visualization, and enter the access code 1010.

Deuteronomy 8:18 reminds us that "It is the Lord that gives us the power to make wealth, that His covenant may be established with us." We are a part of the Abrahamic covenant because of our faith is in the God of Abraham, Isaac and Jacob. This covenant is meant for us to be prosperous and wealthy. Money is not bad. It's the love of money that is the root of all evil (1 Timothy 6:10). Additionally, in Ecclesiastes 9: 10 the scripture tells us that "money answers all things."

This is the word of God and He wants you be wealthy. He wants you to be the solution. He wants you to be lender and not a borrower. The word even says that He wants us to leave an inheritance for our children's children (Proverbs 13:22). He has put in you the power to make wealth.

Close your eyes, breathe deeply, and get into a comfortable position. Allow yourself to think about the ideas that God has implanted in you to make wealth. Perhaps you may have forgotten some of these ideas for various reasons. However, now you are beginning to recall them. Begin to see yourself implementing these ideas. Whether that means going back to school, starting a business, writing a book, getting a certification, starting a social media platform, opening a franchise, now is the time to activate the promise. Whatever it is, begin to see yourself doing it and being successful with it. Begin to visualize your bank account and see it growing. See your finances changing. See God's hand upon you, granting you favor and success in all that you do.

Consider:

Consider writing down those business ideas right here on a piece of paper. Create a timeframe for starting this venture. Do some research, but don't allow it to overwhelm you. Many times, we procrastinate and get caught up on small details because we want to know everything. However, if we knew everything, we could become easily overwhelmed and not do anything at all. So, be well informed, but don't allow it to cause analysis paralysis. Start from somewhere.

Day 7

Prayers over Relationships

The enemy does not like marriages and God-ordained relationships. He wants division because a house divided against itself cannot stand. Therefore, the enemy wants us to not only remain emotionally broken and wounded to transmit trauma, but also for our children to be raised according to negative generational patterns. There are also relationships that are unhealthy and not God-ordained. God does not want any of us experiencing any form of abuse, whether that be mental, emotional, or physical. Nevertheless, change begins with you. If you are not healthy, you won't be healthy for somebody else. God wants to do a new thing in you so that those connected to you can become healthy as well.

Many times, we're focused on those around us, and what they did or are doing. However, remember that it starts with you. For every finger we point there are more fingers pointing right back towards us. I remember being quite defensive in my marriage, as I mentioned before. I would compartmentalize my feelings and withhold communication due to fear of retaliation or rejection. However, this only led to resentment and anger, in which I would implode. My spouse, on the other hand, would communicate in a way that I thought was complaining. My defensiveness then took an all-time high, because I was tired of being seen as wrong based on how I was interpretating his expression concerning the marriage.

I would always pray, "God change him, change him." One day on a fast, I had a supernatural experience where I told God that "Something needed to change in him because he must have bumped his head!" To my surprise, God responded with, "Go wash his feet." I heard this so clear in my head that I knew it wasn't me thinking. "You want me to do what?" God was showing me that change begins with me and I needed to humble myself if I wanted it to happen. I did this and it changed the atmosphere right away – my husband did not know what to do, he was so confused! All he could say was, "I don't deserve this."

That's exactly what love is. It confuses hell and hell's assignment of hatred and division. God shows this to us all the time in the form of mercy, where He doesn't give us what we deserve. The fruit of the Spirit doesn't come just in favorable times; it comes when it's the hardest as well. If everything was happy go lucky, it would be easy to love. However, that love would be superficial. Love is enduring and covers a multitude of wrongs. The disclaimer is that love is not about excusing abuse. Love also sets healthy boundaries as God does not want us in unhealthy abusive relationships of any kind.

What do I do about my current relationship? If you're unsure about the status of your relationship because of the immense number of issues, I do suggest therapy. Individual therapy from a Christian counselor is always a great place to start. As you allow God to do a new thing in you, He will touch everything concerning you. It didn't start with you, but it stops with you.

Prayer:

Thank You, Father, for giving us power and authority to stand in the gap for our children and families. I pray, knowing that these prayers will shift any issue concerning me, my husband, children and our family of origin.

On behalf of my husband, my children, and our families:

Father, there are hurts and disappointments that I've experienced in my current relationships as well as mistakes that I've made in these relationships. I want to forgive. I now recognize that forgiveness is not a feeling but a decision that will allow healing to take place in these current relationships. I forgive those who have hurt and disappointed me. I also forgive myself.

I pray against people-pleasing behavior that comes from not knowing my worth; it also comes from unhealthy views of myself and others, or the fear of setting healthy boundaries.

I pray against putting pressure on myself to look a certain way (that doesn't speak to who I am in Christ) in my social, family or work relationships.

Spirits of confusion and chaos that have caused any disruption, I bind you and command You to go to the pit in Jesus' name!

I divorce any spirit spouse that could be married to me or married to my children from birth. I bind the incubus and succubus spirit, and I command them to go to the bottomless pit and never return in Jesus' name.

I bind the *yandere* (yin-da-ry) spirit (a spirit behind a violent or extreme level of devotion to a love interest), and command it to go to the pit in Jesus' name! Father, help me recognize the differences between a healthy vs unwholesome interest in a person, or in sound relationships vs infatuations.

I bind every familiar spirit that has followed my bloodline, and I command it to go to the pit and never return in Jesus' name.

I bind the spirit of accusation that brings up past mistakes in a voice of condemnation, and I silence that voice that brings up my past and lies about who I am. No one will be moved by your accusations. I command you to go to the pit in Jesus' name!

I bind covenant-breaking spirits, and command these spirits to go to the pit in Jesus' name!

Father, I pray that You show me the areas of my heart that You want to change, and I accept that I am the change that I want to see.

I pray against domestic violence, and I cancel the enemy's assignment of creating toxic relationships in our family and bloodline.

I pray against every agent of satan behind relationships that are sent to derail me. I declare that they fall into their own destruction and traps that they set out for me and those connected to me in Jesus' name.

Father, remove the cords of wicked from us.

Father, remove every destiny destroyer in the mighty name of Jesus. I pray that You connect us to our destiny helpers.

I renounce and cancel cycles and patterns of divorce in my bloodline.

Father, remove every seducer and seductress from our path in Jesus' name.

Father, I pray that any door to past ex's (where no children are involved) or toxic relationships remain closed in Jesus' name.

I pray for healthy co-parenting relationships and healthy interactions where there is a blended family.

I decree that my children will enter into God-fearing covenant-sustaining relationships.

I decree that I, my husband and family always put God first in all of our relationships.

I decree over us that a family that prays together stays together and we are that family.

In my marriage, the three-fold cord is not quickly broken and what God has brought together, let no man put asunder.

I pray against the spirit of pride and selfishness in me, my husband and family. I bind that spirit, and command it to go to the pit in Jesus' name.

I decree that we look for ways to serve each other, as charity begins at home, and love is the greatest.

Lord, bless us to love each other the way You love us, as this is Your commandment.

I decree that we will not look to embarrass each other in private or in public.

Father, help us to be in agreement about raising our children in the way that they should go, so when they are older they will not depart from it (Proverbs 22:6).

I decree that we will not turn our children against each other or take sides.

Father, my conversations and the words that I have used have not always been pleasing in Your eyes. There were times when I have spoken negative words over loved ones and those I didn't know. I do not want to participate in gossip, slander, or use my mouth to speak evil. As Your Prophet Isaiah had to cleanse his lips, because he was a man of unclean lips, I ask You to cleanse my lips and the lips of those around me.

Father, there are times where I've vented about loved ones and spoken carelessly. I understand now that, although I need to express my feelings, it is very important who I do that with, so that my words and expressions lead to a perspective of clarity, wise counsel and peace. Father, I ask that You connect me with the right counsel, and forgive me for speaking idly without no thought of consequences. Father, forgive me for focusing on the flaws of others, when we all have sinned and come short of Your glory, and no one is perfect. However, thank You that You are perfecting everything concerning me and I am here because of Your grace and mercy.

May these words of my mouth and this meditation of my heart be pleasing in Your sight, O Lord, my Rock and my Redeemer (Psalm 19:14).

I decree that we will not look to be defensive or offended, but we will have the courage to have healthy communication.

I decree that we step out of cycles of unhealthy communication and division.

Father, I pray that You help us to manage the responsibilities together in our household.

Father, I pray against taking on more burdens than I can handle (in relationships, at work, etc.), or taking on responsibility for matters that I'm not responsible for. I will not be an enabler, but empower those around me. I pray that You give me the wisdom to recognize what is within my capacity.

I pray against the wrong connections. May the wrong connections be disconnected right now in Jesus' name.

I pray against trauma bonding, unhealthy co-dependent relationships, and relationships that are stagnant or complacent. Father, let them be removed from us now in Jesus' name!

I pray that You give us the gift of discerning of spirits and that we grow in the gift so that we may discern the spirit behind the person.

Father, I thank You for opportunities that You give us to develop the fruit of the Spirit within us which is faithfulness, gentleness, joy, love, peace, kindness, goodness, and patience.

I acknowledge that we develop this fruit through trials and tribulations where we can choose to become offended or we can choose to grow.

Our mindset around offense has shifted, so that we are open to what You are doing in order to break generational patterns of division, divorce, and depression. We will look upon situations that offended us as opportunities to give birth to the fruit of the Spirit.

I thank You, Father, for what You are doing in us and our families. You are the master potter and we are the clay!

I declare that it didn't start with me, but it stops with me!

Scripture:

Ecclesiastes 3:11:
He has made everything beautiful in its time. Also, he has put eternity into man's heart, yet so that he cannot find out what God has done from the beginning to the end.

Visualization: Visit bonus.stopswithyou.com to watch and listen to the visualization, and enter the access code 1010.

Ecclesiastes 3:11 says that God makes everything beautiful in His time. He has put eternity into the heart of man so that he can discover what God has done from beginning to the end. Ecclesiastes also says there is a time for everything, and now is your time for transformation. If we were to remain the way we are or enter into relationships without allowing God to refine us, this can perpetuate patterns of brokenness. Relationships will either remain unresolved or a new relationship will be a repeat of the last one. It's therefore important for us to delight ourselves in the Lord, so that we can handle the desires that are in our hearts and those He wants to give us. No matter where you are in terms of relationships, allowing God to restore you and refine you is going to benefit any relationship that you desire or are connected to already. Remember, when God wants to restore a relationship, He begins with you.

Close your eyes, relax, and get into a comfortable position. Begin to see the areas that God is working on in your life. Allow Him to bring to your mind right now the areas that He is working on and wants to fix. Begin to imagine how He is beautifying you. He is changing you. He is transforming you. Things that used to bother you no longer bother you. See yourself working on your personal growth. See yourself receiving God's love and loving yourself and others from that place.

If there are areas in your life where you lack discipline, such as cleanliness, organization, or health issues, begin to see yourself being intentional about working on these areas. See your house clean. See your car clean. See your work areas clean. See yourself looking your best. See yourself smiling. See yourself receiving the help you need, and growing. He is making you and everything connected to you beautiful. Begin to thank Him from your heart. Thank Him that it is your time. Let this be your meditation.

Consider:

Consider writing down the areas that He's showing you. These are the areas He wants to work on and beautify. What are these areas? Does it have anything to do with the relationship that you have with Him? Does it have anything to do with your emotions? Your health? Organization? Finances? Write them down and be intentional about small changes you can begin to make. You can even focus on one area at a time so that you do not overwhelm yourself. Small steps can lead to consistency. Transformation does not happen overnight; therefore His process of beautifying you will not happen overnight. Consistency over time leads to the transformation that He's already predestined for you. It is your time.

Day 8

Prayers for Healing of Sickness and Infirmity

Many a time, we make sickness a normal part of our being. If we see it in the family medical history, we are fearful that we could have it at some point. That is not your portion. That does not have to happen. I said on the back of this book that even doctors take note of generational patterns so that they can identify what you might be predisposed to. But just because it's been in the family bloodline doesn't mean that you have to endure it. It didn't start with you but it stops with you. No matter the sickness, Christ took thirty-nine lashes so that we can be healed by His stripes.

There are four types of genetic disease categories and within those categories are thirty-nine genetic diseases. Four types are, the single gene inheritance disease, multi-factorial genetic inheritance disorders, chromosome abnormalities, and mitochondrial genetic inheritance disorders. Notice how the word "inheritance" is repeated – wow! Nevertheless, by His grace you have inherited salvation and His healing power is ready to take over you and your bloodline. Jesus our Lord and Savior took thirty-nine lashes so every disease can be destroyed and you are not destroyed.

Prayer:

Father, thank You for giving us power and authority to stand in the gap for our children and families. I pray, knowing that these prayers will shift any issue concerning me, my husband, children and our families.

On behalf of my husband, my children and families of origin:

Father, have mercy upon us and cleanse us from all unrighteousness, iniquity, transgressions, and sin from us and those that came before us.

I bind every spirit of infirmity impacting my bloodline, and command it to go to the pit of hell in Jesus' name.

I bind the spirit of gluttony, and command it to go to the pit in Jesus' name!

Father, I acknowledge that I haven't always taken care of my body and treated it like the temple it is. Give me the wisdom and resources to make better choices and buy the healthiest food.

I bind the spirit of death and premature death, and command it to go to the pit of hell in Jesus' name.

I decree that we will not go before our time!

Father, there are times where I've relied on outside motivation or my feelings, and did not exercise as a result of this. Please help me to build consistency in physical exercise, and maintain it.

I take authority over our body and our bloodline, and command every known and unknown disease to come out of us and go back to the pit of hell in Jesus' name.

As I command the following thirty-nine genetic disorders to leave, I am also commanding all the spirits and diseases that fall under these genetic disorders to leave in Jesus' name!

I command cystic fibrosis, sickle cell anemia and marfan syndrome to leave my bloodline now and go to the pit of hell in Jesus' name.

I command douchenne muscular dystrophy, huntington disease, polycystic kidney disease types one and two, and tay-sachs disease to leave my bloodline now and go to the pit of hell in Jesus' name.

I command phenylketonuria, maple syrup urine disease, neurofibromatosis type 1, to leave my bloodline now and go to the pit of hell in Jesus' name.

I command alpha-1 antitrypsin deficiency, galactosemia, familial hyper cholesterolemia, and red syndrome to come out of my bloodline now and go to the pit of hell in Jesus' name.

I command hemophilia, fanconi anemia, kartagener syndrome, and xeroderma pigmentosum to come out of my bloodline now and go to the pit of hell in Jesus' name amen.

I command hereditary spherocytosis, tuberous sclerosis, von hippel-lindau syndrome to come out of my bloodline now and go to the pit of hell in Jesus' name.

I command down syndrome, cri-du-chat syndrome, klinefelter syndrome, patau syndrome, and edwards syndrome to come out of my bloodline now and go to the pit of hell in Jesus' name.

I command turner syndrome, 22q112 deletion syndrome, ring chromosome 14 syndrome, Prader-Willi syndrome and hereditary optic atrophy to leave my bloodline now and go to the pit of hell in Jesus' name.

I command barth syndrome, co-enzyme Q10 deficiency, myoclonic epilepsy with raised red fibers, and MELAS syndrome (a rare form of dementia) to come out of my bloodline now and go to the pit of hell in Jesus' name.

I command Kearns-Sayre syndrome, Pearson syndrome, neuropathy, ataxia, retinitis Pigmentosa and Leigh's disease to come out of my bloodline and go to the pit of hell in Jesus' name amen.

Father, I rejoice knowing that You have healed me, my husband and children and our bloodline. I decree that my doctors will be astonished by my health report! Our health is restored to Your intended purpose! I thank You for our healing and our freedom!

I declare that it didn't start with me, but it stops with me!

Scripture:

Isaiah 53:5 NKJV:

He was wounded for our transgressions, He was bruised for our iniquities; the chastisement for our peace was upon Him, and by His stripes we are healed.

Visualization: Visit bonus.stopswithyou.com to watch and listen to the visualization, and enter the access code 1010.

Isaiah 53:5 says He was wounded for our transgressions; He was bruised for our iniquities; the punishment for our peace was upon Him, and by His stripes we are healed. Jesus took thirty-nine lashes which, by no coincidence, covers the thirty-nine genetic disorders that all diseases come from. Illnesses or diseases traveling through your bloodline is not your portion. God's healing power is already at work as you have commanded those diseases to depart from you and your bloodline, whether you knew or didn't know they were a part of your medical history.

When Jesus healed the sick, He asked them if they believed they could be healed. Therefore, your faith in what He has already done is key to receiving the full manifestation of your healing. There is a story of Jesus healing ten lepers in Luke chapter 17. After this, He asked them to show themselves to the priest (as was the law) to validate the healing. They all went but only one of them returned to thank Him. The others did not return to say thanks but they were healed nonetheless. Many times, we're not fully grateful for what God has done and slip into our normal routine, even places that are harmful. However, God wants not only to heal you but for you to follow after Him, as there is more that He wants to do for you.

You see, when the healed leper returned, Jesus told him his faith had made him whole. You can see there's a difference between healing and wholeness. While the healing may be physical, wholeness affects your entire body and soul. "He who the Son sets free is free indeed" (John 8:36). You are healed by the blood of Jesus, and He has cleansed your bloodline. Close your eyes, breathe deeply and settle yourself. Begin to see yourself and those connected to you standing together. See the light of God coming from His throne, which is beginning to overshadow you and enter you. Begin to watch as the shadow of sickness departs from you and your bloodline. See it as something dark that is leaving you and your bloodline. Because of the light of God, which encompasses His healing power and love, the darkness of sickness and infirmity cannot remain, and it has to return to where you command it to go. See yourself thanking God for your healing and following His instruction and direction. Not only are you healed, but your faith has made you whole. As you meditate on this, you will feel His presence all over you.

Consider:

Consider areas in your health and wellness that need Improvement. Write down the changes that you want to make so that you can take care of your body which is the temple of the Holy Spirit. As we have believed God for healing, we do not want to put junk in our bodies and be lackadaisical about exercise. Do you need to meet with a nutritionist? Do you need to join a support group around food, like weight watchers? Do you need a personal trainer? It helps to connect to a person and receive ongoing support for health changes, if needed.

Day 9

Prayers for Restoration of What Was Stolen or Lost and Fulfillment of God's Plan

God wants to restore what has been taken from your bloodline. Do you know there were assignments, projects, rewards and inheritances, amongst other things, that those who came before you were meant to receive or complete? They didn't due to the enemy's deception. Some spirits behind this are the Pharaoh spirit and a Lilith spirit (that kills things in infancy or beginnings), a jailer spirit (its operation is to lock you and your progress) or other assassination spirits who want to steal or kill your children, assignments, and opportunities. The enemy is after your time and cause disruption, so we end up wasting time. The enemy wants you to be broken, but you have been chosen to be the generational curse breaker.

Sometimes, we underestimate how short life is. James 4:14 describes our life as like a vapor, here one day gone the next. The enemy wants you to be stuck in the past or have a stubborn mindset, so you do not move forward or prosper. Just as he is condemned, he wants you to be mentally and emotionally crippled so that you are not cultivated to grow into the person God has called you to be. That is why he uses people to attack each other to keep us distracted by the person and our pain, and consequently step out of our purpose. However, you are meant to be great, and not nursing your grief!

Myles Munroe once said that the richest place is a cemetery. Here there are paintings that were never painted, books that were never written, and designs that were never created because people died before they fulfilled their potential. It's time for you to rob the grave and reclaim what is yours. God can restore what has been stolen and cause supernatural speed and acceleration to come upon you along with His strength, so that you fulfill His plan and purpose for your life.

Prayer:

Father, thank You for giving us power and authority to stand in the gap for our husbands, children and families. I pray, knowing that these prayers will shift any issue concerning me, my husband, children and our families.

On behalf of my husband, our children and our families:

I bind the spirit of Pharoh (that causes death in infancy or early beginnings) that has come up against our bloodline, children and assignments, and command it to go to the pit in Jesus' name.

I bind the spirit of Lilith (spirit behind infant death), that comes against children. I command that spirit to go to the pit in Jesus' name, amen.

I bind the spirit of Jezebel (manipulative spirit, misdirection spirit, and assassination spirit of assignments/purpose), and command it to go to the pit in Jesus' name.

You jailer spirit, who comes to lock me or my progress, I command You to loose my finances, my career, and anything connected to my destiny or progress. I command you to go to the pit in Jesus' name!

I bind the spirit of confusion, and command our minds and our destinies to be completely loosed in Jesus' name.

I bind every serpent and scorpion against us, and command them to go to the pit in Jesus' name.

I bind the spirit of divination and seducing spirits against us, and command them to go to the pit in Jesus' name.

I bind any spirit of limitation, and command it to go to the pit in Jesus' name.

Father, I bind the spirit behind miscarriages of children and of ideas that You have placed in us, and I command it to go to the pit in Jesus' name. I pray that You give us beauty for ashes, joy for mourning.

I bind you strong man (dominant spirit that controls smaller spirits) and I bind all your host! I command you all to go to the pit in Jesus' name!

Father, send the hornet among the enemies that block or remain in places that belong to me, until those that are left hiding are destroyed in Jesus' name! (Deuteronomy 7:20)

Father, let every curse or rap that the enemy wants for us, fall on them instead!

I cancel all injuries and accidents in Jesus' name!

I pray against and cancel illegal activities, incarceration, jail, and imprisonment of me or anyone connected to me. We will not fall into foolish situations. Father, order our steps!

I cancel any words of limitation that have been spoken over me, my husband, our children and our destinies.

I pray against and cancel barrenness in Jesus' name!

I decree that we are fruitful in everything that we do.

Father, make us prosper in every area of our lives. I declare that we will be successful.

Father, I ask that You bless the works of our hands.

Father, I thank You for breaking generational curses, and ask that You restore everything that has been stolen in health, finances, relationships and assignments.

Father, I ask that You have compassion on us and put the pieces back together that were broken and scattered in every area of our lives.

I reclaim my marriage, children, finances, grants, scholarships, land, buildings, books, houses and mansions, cars, businesses, inventions, songs, record deals, rewards and recognitions, promotions, bonuses, commissions, and other creative exploits or opportunities that were lost.

I pray that You remind us of any ideas that You had given us that we had forgotten or neglected.

I decree that we will no longer undermine our gifts or bury them.

I decree that we will not allow people to destroy us from fulfilling the ideas that You have given us.

Father, I ask for wisdom concerning who to share our dreams or ideas with.

I decree that we are putting our trust in the Lord because You know the plans that You have for us and those plans are to prosper us.

I decree that my children will be top performers in school and out of school, and we shall all have a spirit of excellence in everything we do.

I decree that I and my children are brilliant and creative and I will speak life into them daily.

Father, please restore the time; I pray for supernatural speed and acceleration.

Father, I thank You and praise You for what has already been done!

I declare that it didn't start with me, but it stops with me!

Scripture:

Jeremiah 29:11 NKJV:

For I know the thoughts that I think toward you, says the Lord, thoughts of peace and not of evil, to give you a future and a hope.

Visualization: Visit bonus.stopswithyou.com to watch and listen to the visualization, and enter the access code 1010.

Jeremiah 29:11 says that God knows the plans that He has for you and that He wants to prosper you, not harm you. Child of God, your future is bright. Truly there is greatness on the inside of you. There is potential that is waiting to come forth. God has chosen you to be the generational curse breaker. The enemy's continuous stealing from your bloodline ends with you because you have said yes to being a warrior and a vessel for the mighty things that God is going to do through you.

Close your eyes, inhale deeply and get in a comfortable position. Begin to see those things that were stolen being returned to you: your peace, finances, children, businesses, land, ideas, or marriage. Whatever it is, see it being returned to you seven times. See God sending His angels before you, clearing the way for you so that wherever you go, you will prosper. See yourself with a renewed confidence because your trust is in Him. There's a light coming from His throne. See it shining on you very brightly as you begin to experience His presence. This light and His presence is with you and everything concerning you. Let this be your meditation.

Consider:

As a prophetic action (activated faith in movement), consider making a list of what has to be reclaimed and restored. Revisit the list and check the items off, as you experience the manifestation.

Day 10

Prayers for Perseverance and Rest

Praise God for doing a mighty work in your life and those connected to you! You are a kingdom builder! Your obedience to your calling and fulfilling your purpose is the key to someone else's freedom. If you don't make it, they won't make it. It's that serious! Many times, when we receive a prophetic word, and we declare change to happen in our lives, or we may have started a business/projects. But we become discouraged when we don't see it right away.

Understand that you have shifted your family's trajectory in a significant way. The enemy is trembling right now because he has lost his hold on you. Remember, when he wants you to be discouraged and delayed, he plants seeds of doubt and creates disruption so that you lose your focus. His goal is to slow you down or stop you so that you abandon your assignment. Do not be deceived. Do not be deceived. Do not be deceived.

Know that, if your sins, mistakes, tribulations were too big for God, He wouldn't be God. He knew everything you'd do and what storms would come your way. However, in order to experience peace and persevere, you must keep your mind on Him and learn how to receive His rest in the midst of the storm. So, rest, knowing that God has put in you everything that you need to do to be successful. Rest is knowing that, as you remain in Him, nothing can stand before you to oppose you. If God is for you, who can be against you? (Romans 8:13) No one.

Everything that you have experienced up into this moment and things to come are only to reveal who God is to you. He wants intimacy with you and He wants you to know who you are in Him. He wants you to run your race well and persevere. I remember going through very hard seasons, praying, and not seeing change happen right-away. Sometimes I'd see some change and then I'd experience the same circumstances again. The enemy was trying to play with my mind so that I would doubt and speak negative words. One time, I discerned the enemy speaking lies into my ear even while I was writing this book. The deceiving spirit said, "Stop, you're not delivered. Stop writing."

Are you surprised a spirit can do this? Who said that just because you are Holy Ghost filled the enemy won't come around? Jesus fasted for forty days and the devil still came and tempted Him because He wanted to misdirect Jesus' assignment by getting Him to "prove Himself" or demonstrate evidence of His sonship. To have Jesus worship him, he promised he would give Jesus the kingdom (as if Jesus didn't already have the kingdom!) However, the Lord Jesus had a word in season that canceled the enemy's assignment.

The enemy comes around so he can misdirect you with lies to think there's a microwaved way. He wants you to compare yourself with others, which usually leaves people feeling inadequate. They then want "proof" that the plan or the dream they have will actually work, leaving them in angst or analysis paralysis if they see nothing. The devil also wants you to worship him. He plays on our worries that things are not happening fast enough. He knows we want instant gratification instead of enduring or persevering.

"I would never worship Him," you may say. Well, whatever you give your attention to is a form of worship. Worrying is worship, because it consumes you and takes your attention off your assignment. The devil comes when you feel vulnerable as well. Ya'll, I felt its presence strongly and I began to stand on my authority. I literally moved from a sitting position and stood up. I was serious, but I said, "La, la, la, la, la, I'm not listening to you. Go away, devil! Not today or any day!" The spirit has left because it lost its assignment, instead of me losing my focus and my assignment. There's still much for me to accomplish!

Pause for a praise break! Death and life are in the power of the tongue (Proverbs 18:21). You can either speak life or death into a situation that actually needs life. God was teaching me His ways so I could know His faithfulness. He was teaching me to be faithful with what He's given me. He has put something in you that you need to give birth to. People are not perfect and will disappoint you, but God is perfect and faithful. He is a covenant-keeping God, and He does not lie. His word does not return void. You must not give up. Do not let the enemy's disruptions discourage you. Keep going, and allow God to develop you. The key to overcoming those obstacles is being reliant on His strength and continuing to speak life as you run your race.

Lastly, when Jesus and the disciples were on the boat, there was a storm. Jesus was asleep while His disciples were terrified. The disciples woke Him up and asked if He even cared that they were drowning, and Jesus rebuked the storm, saying, "Peace be still." The storm was sent to disrupt His peace. Those around Him were doubtful showing they were also peace disrupters, and He rebuked them for their little faith. Be discerning of peace disrupters, and use wisdom to protect your peace.

Additionally, your faith is not meant to remain a mustard seed. When that storm hits you (in a relationship, finances, business, books, ministry, etc.), remember what I said. Remain calm and plug into God's rest because there is no peace without the Prince of Peace. It's easy to be happy when everything is all good BUT AS EASY AS THAT IS … it will be easy to become disoriented, dismantled, and discouraged if you do not know how to receive true peace from the only One that can give it to you.

When you experience that true genuine peace in the midst of the storm, the devil can use nothing – I repeat, NOTHING – to disrupt you because you know the true peace to persevere!

Prayer:

Father, thank You for giving us power and authority to stand in the gap for our husbands, children and families. I pray, knowing that these prayers will shift any issue concerning me, my husband, children and families.

On behalf of my husband, my children and our families:

Father, I thank You that I am forgiven for every sin. Thank You for cleaning me and renewing my mind, consciously and subconsciously. I am free and cleansed by the precious blood of Jesus.

Nothing that I have ever done is stopping You from using me now and in the future. I submit completely to You and give You my whole heart.

I thank You that I am a new creature in Christ!

Father, there are times where I experience thoughts of doubt or unbelief. Just as You did with the man who asked You to help his unbelief (Mark 9:24), I pray that You give me the grace to overcome my unbelief. I decree that I will not allow any negative thoughts to spiral, but I will instead cast them down and make them obedient to Jesus Christ.

Father, remove the thorns (which choke God's word or encouraging words) from our hearts in Jesus' name.

Father, remove any hardened parts (stubborn mindsets that don't yield) in our hearts, and give us a heart of flesh.

Father, make me good soil so that Your word takes root within me and those connected to me.

Father, help us to recognize that our feelings fluctuate. We will not lean on our own understanding, but we will allow You to lead us into all truth!

Father, give us the ability to filter information that comes in through our minds and help us to decipher Your voice.

I decree that You are the Potter and we are the clay. Mold us into who You have called us to be. We thank You that You will not stop until Jesus returns.

Father, I receive the complete work of the cross.

Father, I ask that You continue to order our steps.

I declare that I and my bloodline will give birth to everything that You have deposited within us.

Father, I declare that every cycle of hindrance and delay is broken off us and our bloodline right now in Jesus' name.

Father, we thank You for stability in You.

Father, I now understand that the storms that come are not to make me drown or give up. I decree that I will not give up and I will count it all joy when there are storms, trials and tribulations happening around me because they help me to become strong and mature (James 1:2-4). I will persevere so I am not lacking in growth in the places You want to take me.

I will not allow the circumstances of life to make me a complainer. Instead, I will practice gratitude daily!

Father, I now know that leaning on my own understanding brings about stagnancy because dwelling on the probability of failure or what looks impossible is the opposite of faith. Give me wisdom, understanding and knowledge so that I may establish everything I build – including relationships, businesses, and finances – on a solid foundation. I now know that I will also receive rare and beautiful treasures as a result of this! (Proverbs 24:3-4)

I will focus on God who keeps us in perfect peace if our minds are stayed on You (Isaiah 26:3).

Father, Your word says that we will find You when we seek You with all of our heart (Jeremiah 29:13). We give You all of our heart right now because You are our source.

Father, show us how to find rest in You in spite of the storms.

Father, Your word says faith comes by hearing and hearing by the word of God (Romans 10:17). Therefore, perseverance and faith are connected to my hearing Your word, not just when I read the bible, but through my spirit on a daily basis. However, I have struggled to hear Your voice at times because other voices in my mind are too loud. Give me the grace to mute and silence the enemy. Give me the grace to be quiet not only on the outside, but in my mind so that I may hear Your voice and receive comfort, correction, and direction.

Father, I acknowledge that I now understand that rest is also knowing that everything works together for the good of them that love God and are called according to their purpose (Romans 8:28). Because I love You and am called into my purpose, whatever I'm facing will have a good outcome!

In You, we live move and have our being, which is the key to persevering through all odds (Acts 17:28).

Father, as Your word says, we are surrounded by a great cloud of witnesses, so I know heaven is backing me. I will throw off everything that hinders me and the sin that so easily entangles me. I will run the race that You have marked out for me (and no longer compare myself with others) and I will do it with perseverance! (Hebrews 12:1-2)

Father, thank You for giving me an understanding heart!

Thank You for helping me to resist any temptation to quit!

I thank You that I can do all things through Christ who gives me strength (Philippians 4:13).

Jesus, be exalted in me, my husband, children and our families.

I thank You, that it is not by our might or our power but by Your strength that we can fulfill all that You've called us to be in Jesus' name!

I declare that it didn't start with me, but it stops with me!

Scripture:

Ezekiel 37:1-10 NIV:

The hand of the LORD was on me, and he brought me out by the Spirit of the LORD and set me in the middle of a valley; it was full of bones. He led me back and forth among them, and I saw a great many bones on the floor of the valley, bones that were very dry. e asked me, "Son of man, can these bones live?"

I said, "Sovereign LORD, you alone know."

Then he said to me, "Prophesy to these bones and say to them, 'Dry bones, hear the word of the LORD! This is what the Sovereign LORD says to these bones: I will make breath enter you, and you will come to life. I will attach tendons to you and make flesh come upon you and cover you with skin; I will put breath in you, and you will come to life. Then you will know that I am the LORD.'"

So I prophesied as I was commanded. And as I was prophesying, there was a noise, a rattling sound, and the bones came together, bone to bone. I looked, and tendons and flesh appeared on them and skin covered them, but there was no breath in them.

Then he said to me, "Prophesy to the breath; prophesy, son of man, and say to it, 'This is what the Sovereign LORD says: Come, breath, from the four winds and breathe into these slain, that they may live.'" So I prophesied as he commanded me, and breath entered them; they came to life and stood up on their feet — a vast army.

Visualization: Visit bonus.stopswithyou.com to watch and listen to the visualization, and enter the access code 1010.

The bible tells us the faith comes by hearing, and hearing by the word of God. Prophesying God's word and walking in faith, (inspite of what's happening), is key to your perseverance and rest. Ezekiel 37:1-10 is showing us the encounter that God had with this prophet. You are the best prophet of your life. A prophet essentially speaks God's perfect will into the situation and calls for what already exists but has not yet manifested physically. God, who is all knowing, asked Ezekiel if those Dry Bones, which seemed hopeless and lifeless, could live. Although God knows the end from the beginning, He did this to cause Ezekiel to reappraise the situation, not from his limited understanding but from the understanding that when God tells us to speak to a situation, anything is possible. Therefore, faith in God's word and speaking God's word inspite of what's happening around you, will help you endure, persevere, and have rest because you know everything is working together for your good.

He wanted Ezekiel to be decisive with this revelation. The only thing that's standing between you and the great destiny that God has for you is your decision. Either you speak life into it or death. You must decide, and that's why God did it this way. Every circumstance in your life is God having an encounter with you just like He did with Ezekiel. You must decide to focus on the outcome and not the opposition. When you speak life, the opposition has to move out of your way.

When Ezekiel prophesied over the bones, the breath of God came into them, and turned them from a lifeless mass into a strong army. In the same way, James 1:2-3 says, "Consider it pure joy, my brothers and sisters, whenever you face trials of all sorts because you know that the testing of your faith produces perseverance." Therefore, another key to persevering is understanding that your pain is not in vain. Pain is priceless to God, and He will allow that pain so that you give birth to what He has deposited in you. Just like a woman in labor, the birthing is painful, but there's nothing but pure joy at what you have given birth to.

Therefore, focus on the voice that is telling you to push through, push, push, push; don't give up, don't give up! Close your eyes, take a deep breath and make yourself comfortable. Begin to see yourself speaking life over everything concerning you, even seemingly dead situations. As you speak, watch the words become light that are released from your mouth. The light of your words goes into that situation and transforms it. Then begin to see those situations change and work in your favor as the power of God and the breath of God is carried in your words. Let this be your meditation.

Consider:

Consider writing down what has been prophesied over you or what you have prophesied over.

Make daily declarations and deeds (tasks that you're supposed to be doing in the process), and watch the manifestation happen!

Congratulations on completing this book! This is the beginning of God shifting the course of your bloodline and those that are connected to you. You are a committed believer and God will keep His Covenant. You are blessed and highly favored. Your portion in God is great. What the enemy meant for evil, God will turn around for good. Everything is working together for your good.

I encourage you to continue to be intentional about your meeting time with God. Have private time with God for yourself. If you have a family, continue to have a dedicated time of prayer. If you've identified therapy or counseling as beneficial for you, be intentional about getting it started. This is your time to live life abundantly and believe that God is making you, your husband, your children and those connected to you beautiful. Rejoice, my sister, knowing that you have won!

Biblical revelations behind the number 10

When the Lord gave me 10:10, I knew in my spirit that this was a prophetic sign. Not only does it refer to John 10:10, "*The thief does not come except to steal, and to kill, and to destroy. I have come that they may have life, and that they may have it more abundantly,*" but it speaks to the significance of the double 10.

These points highlight the symbolic and practical significance of the number 10 throughout the Bible.

- **Ten Commandments**: Given to Moses on Mount Sinai, these are the fundamental laws for Israel and the new covenant church (Exodus 20:1-17).

- **Ten Plagues of Egypt**: God sent ten plagues upon Egypt to convince Pharaoh to release the Israelites from slavery (Exodus 7-12).

- **Tithing**: The Israelites were commanded to give a tenth (tithe) of their produce to support the Levites, the poor, and the temple (Leviticus 27:30-32).

- **Ten Generations from Adam to Noah**: This genealogical sequence highlights the early history of mankind (Genesis 5).

- **Parable of the Ten Virgins**: In the New Testament, Jesus uses this parable to teach about being prepared for the Kingdom of Heaven (Matthew 25:1-13).

- **Ten Lepers Cleansed**: Jesus heals ten lepers, emphasizing gratitude and faith (Luke 17:11-19).

- **Ten Days of Testing**: In the Book of Revelation, the church in Smyrna is told they will face ten days of testing (Revelation 2:10).

- **Ten Horns and Ten Crowns**: This prophetic vision is symbolic of the beast in Revelation, who represents kingdoms and authority (Revelation 13:1).

- **Ten Spies' Negative Report**: Out of twelve spies sent to scout the Promised Land, ten gave a negative report, leading to Israel's wandering (Numbers 13-14).

- **Jacob's Wages Changed Ten Times**: Laban changed Jacob's wages ten times, reflecting persistence and God's provision (Genesis 31:7).

Index

This is a list of modern-day generational curses and patterns. This can be a valuable resource for understanding how various negative behaviors, beliefs, and circumstances can be perpetuated through families and communities. The way you can use this list is by looking at it one day at a time. Renounce the curse or pattern that applies to you and your family, while stating the definition. Then pray a prayer of faith that affirms God's perfect will preventing that cycle from happening. Remember, even if it's something you don't struggle with, you are renouncing it on behalf of your bloodline. As you go through it each day, cross it out! This is also symbolic of your canceling the cycle because you are a generational curse breaker!

For example: "I renounce all addictions, recurrent substance abuse or dependency on alcohol and drugs. God, fill every void in my life and give me the grace to depend on you, that I may also be healed and soberminded."

Here is the list with definitions:

1. **Addiction**: Recurrent substance abuse or dependency (alcohol, drugs, etc.)
2. **Abuse**: Physical, emotional, or sexual abuse perpetuated across generations
3. **Neglect**: Failure to provide basic needs and emotional support
4. **Poverty**: Chronic financial instability and lack of resources
5. **Divorce**: High incidence of marital breakdown and separation
6. **Domestic Violence**: Patterns of controlling, aggressive, or violent behavior
7. **Mental Illness**: Recurring mental health issues such as depression, anxiety, etc.
8. **Obesity**: Persistent unhealthy eating habits and lack of exercise leading to excessive weight
9. **Poor Education**: Low educational attainment and lack of emphasis on schooling
10. **Criminal Behavior**: Repeated engagement in illegal activities
11. **Teen Pregnancy**: High rates of pregnancy among teenagers

12. **Unemployment**: Chronic joblessness and lack of career stability.

13. **Debt**: Cycles of financial indebtedness and poor money management

14. **Infidelity**: Patterns of cheating and unfaithfulness in relationships

15. **Homelessness**: Lack of stable housing and recurring displacement

16. **Gang Involvement**: Participation in gang activities and related violence

17. **Low Self-Esteem**: Persistent feelings of inadequacy and lack of confidence.

18. **Codependency**: Excessive emotional or psychological reliance on a partner

19. **Eating Disorders**: Disordered eating behaviors, such as anorexia or bulimia

20. **Racism**: Enduring prejudiced beliefs and discriminatory behaviors

21. **Sexism**: Perpetuation of gender-based discrimination and biases

22. **Religious Extremism**: Radical beliefs leading to intolerance and violence

23. **Substance Abuse**: Chronic misuse of drugs or alcohol

24. **Workaholism**: Compulsive overworking to the detriment of personal life

25. **Depression**: Persistent sadness and lack of interest in life activities

26. **Anxiety**: Chronic worry, nervousness, and fear

27. **Isolation**: Social withdrawal and lack of meaningful connections

28. **Suicide**: History of suicidal thoughts or actions within a family

29. **Anger Issues**: Uncontrolled rage and frequent outbursts

30. **Narcissism**: Pattern of self-centered, arrogant behavior

31. **Control Issues**: Compulsive need to control others or situations

32. **Manipulation**: Persistent deceit and exploitation of others

33. **Gambling**: Chronic gambling addiction leading to financial ruin

34. **Detachment**: Emotional disconnection from others

35. **Xenophobia**: Fear or hatred of foreigners or strangers

36. **Perfectionism**: Obsessive striving for flawlessness and setting high standards

37. **Fear of Failure**: Overwhelming fear of making mistakes or failing

38. **Procrastination**: Chronic delay or avoidance of tasks and responsibilities

39. **Judgmental Attitudes**: Constantly criticizing and condemning others

40. **Blame Shifting**: Avoiding personal responsibility by blaming others.

41. **Victim Mentality**: Perceiving oneself as perpetually victimized

42. **Entitlement**: Belief that one deserves special treatment or privileges

43. **Hypercritical Nature**: Excessively finding fault in others

44. **Materialism**: Placing higher value on material possessions over relationships

45. **Pessimism**: Chronic negative outlook on life

46. **Indecisiveness**: Inability to make decisions promptly or confidently

47. **People-Pleasing**: Compulsive need to satisfy others at one's own expense

48. **Gossiping**: Spreading rumors and talking negatively about others

49. **Jealousy**: Envious feelings towards others' success or possessions

50. **Obsessive-Compulsive Behavior**: Repetitive, compulsive actions or thoughts

51. **Hyperactivity**: Excessive activity and difficulty focusing

52. **Apathy**: Lack of interest, enthusiasm, or concern

53. **Passivity**: Reluctance to take action or make decisions.

54. **Reclusiveness**: Avoiding social interaction and secluding oneself

55. **Lying**: Habitual dishonesty or deceit

56. **Cheating**: Engaging in dishonest behavior to gain advantage

57. **Stealing**: Taking what belongs to others without permission

58. **Deceit**: Intentionally misleading others

59. **Enabling**: Supporting harmful behavior in others

60. **Pride**: Excessive self-esteem or arrogance

61. **Unforgiveness**: Holding grudges and unwillingness to forgive

62. **Bitterness**: Resentful and cynical outlook on life

63. **Resentment**: Persistent feelings of being wronged or treated unfairly

64. **Mistrust**: Difficulty trusting others

65. **Inferiority Complex**: Persistent feeling of being less valuable than others

66. **Superiority Complex**: Belief that one is better than others

67. **Passive-Aggressiveness**: Indirect expression of hostility or anger

68. **Sabotaging Relationships**: Deliberately undermining or ending relationships

69. **Fear of Intimacy**: Avoiding close, personal relationships

70. **Obsession**: Fixation on certain thoughts or behaviors

71. **Hypervigilance**: Excessive alertness and suspicion

72. **Persecution Complex**: Belief that one is constantly being persecuted

73. **Hoarding**: Compulsive accumulation of items and inability to discard them

74. **Perfectionist Parenting**: Imposing unrealistic expectations on children

75. **Lack of Boundaries**: Difficulty establishing personal limits

76. **Emotional Distance**: Inability to connect emotionally with others.

77. **Fear of Abandonment**: Anxiety about being left alone or rejected

78. **Overprotectiveness**: Excessive guarding and controlling of loved ones

79. **Overindulgence**: Providing excessive rewards or material goods

80. **Helicopter Parenting**: Over-involvement in children's lives

81. **Inconsistent Discipline**: Erratic enforcement of rules and boundaries

82. **Authoritarianism**: Strict and punitive parenting or leadership style

83. **Negativism**: Persistent negative attitude and resistance to change

84. **Conformity**: Reluctance to think independently or challenge norms

85. **Intolerance**: Unwillingness to accept different viewpoints or behaviors

86. **Rage**: Intense and uncontrolled anger

87. **Martyrdom**: Self-sacrificing behavior to gain sympathy or admiration

88. **Complaining**: Chronic dissatisfaction and verbalizing grievances

89. **Hypochondria**: Excessive worry about having serious illness

90. **Defensiveness**: Reacting protectively or aggressively to criticism

91. **Revenge-Seeking**: Desire to retaliate or harm others for perceived wrongs

92. **Sexual Dysfunction in marriage**: Persistent issues with sexual performance or desire

93. **Financial Irresponsibility**: Poor money management and spending habits

94. **Overconsumption**: Excessive use or consumption of goods and services

95. **Scapegoating**: Blaming one person for the faults of others

96. **Overconfidence**: Excessive belief in one's abilities or judgment

97. **Underachievement**: Failing to reach one's potential due to lack of effort

98. **Chronic Fatigue**: Persistent tiredness and lack of energy

99. **Perfectionist Work Ethic**: Overworking and striving for flawlessness

100. **Attention-Seeking**: Compulsive need for admiration and validation

101. **Lack of Empathy**: Inability to understand or share others' feelings

102. **Stubbornness**: Inflexibility and unwillingness to change

103. **Fear of Success**: Anxiety about achieving and maintaining success

104. **Overreliance on Technology**: Dependence on devices and digital tools

105. **Hypersexuality**: Excessive focus on sexual activity

106. **Sexual Repression**: Suppression of sexual desires and expression

107. **Insecurity**: Persistent feelings of inadequacy and self-doubt

108. **Guilt**: Excessive or chronic feelings of guilt and remorse

109. **Shame**: Persistent feelings of worthlessness and disgrace

110. **Control Freak**: Excessive need to control situations and people.

111. **Fear of Change**: Anxiety about new situations and resistance to change

112. **Rigidity**: Inability to adapt or be flexible

113. **Dependency**: Excessive reliance on others for support or decision-making

114. **Unresolved Grief**: Inability to process and move on from loss

115. **Denial**: Refusal to acknowledge reality or accept facts

116. **Unrealistic Expectations**: Setting impractical standards for oneself or others

117. **Overcommitting**: Taking on too many responsibilities and tasks

118. **Undercommitting**: Avoiding responsibilities and tasks

119. **Chronic Illness**: Recurring health issues within a family

20. **Stress**: Persistent and excessive stress and tension

121. **Burnout**: Exhaustion due to prolonged stress and overwork

122. **Envy**: Desiring what others have and feeling discontented

123. **Laziness**: Avoiding work and productive activities

124. **Indulgence**: Excessive gratification of desires

125. **Overeating**: Consuming food in excessive amounts

126. **Injustice**: Perpetuating unfair treatment and inequity

127. **Prejudice**: Preconceived opinions not based on reason or experience

128. **Bigotry**: Intolerance towards those who are different

129. **Bullying**: Intimidation and harassment of others

130. **Arrogance**: Overbearing pride and self-importance

131. **Cynicism**: Belief that people are motivated purely by self-interest

132. **Mediocrity**: Settling for average and not striving for excellence

133. **Aloofness**: Being distant and detached from others

134. **Frugality**: Extreme and excessive thriftiness

135. **Greed**: Intense and selfish desire for wealth or power

136. **Selfishness**: Concern for oneself at the expense of others

137. **Vanity**: Excessive pride in one's appearance or achievements

138. **Idolatry**: Excessive devotion to or reverence for someone or something

139. **Distrust**: Suspicion and lack of trust in others

140. **Lust**: Intense and uncontrolled sexual desire

141. **Gluttony**: Habitual greed or excess in eating

142. **Sloth**: Reluctance to work or make an effort; laziness

143. **Wrath**: Extreme anger and desire for vengeance

144. **Complacency**: Self-satisfaction with one's achievements leading to lack of effort

145. **Avarice**: Extreme greed for wealth or material gain

146. **Profligacy**: Reckless wastefulness in the use of resources

147. **Intemperance**: Lack of moderation or restraint

148. **Covetousness**: Yearning to possess something belonging to someone else

149. **Impulsiveness**: Acting without thinking or considering consequences

150. **Overanalysis**: Excessive examination or consideration of details

151. **Suspicion**: Mistrust or doubt about someone's intentions

152. **Ingratitude**: Lack of appreciation or thankfulness

153. **Vengefulness**: Desire to retaliate or get back at others

154. **Evasiveness**: Avoiding direct answers or actions

155. **Obfuscation**: Deliberately making something unclear or difficult to understand

156. **Procrastination**: Delaying tasks and responsibilities

157. **Disorganization**: Lack of structure and order in life

158. **Self-Deprecation**: Excessive belittling or undervaluing oneself

159. **Self-Sabotage**: Undermining one's own success or happiness

160. **Despair**: Complete loss of hope

161. **Melancholy**: Persistent sadness or gloominess

162. **Impatience**: Lack of patience or tolerance

163. **Frustration**: Feelings of irritation and dissatisfaction

164. **Sarcasm**: Use of irony to mock or convey contempt

165. **Cynicism**: Belief that people are motivated purely by self-interest

166. **Stoicism**: Endurance of pain or hardship without complaint

167. **Indifference**: Lack of interest, concern, or sympathy

168. **Ruthlessness**: Lack of compassion or empathy

169. **Cruelty**: Willfully causing pain or suffering to others

170. **Sadism**: Deriving pleasure from inflicting pain or suffering

171. **Masochism**: Deriving pleasure from one's own pain or humiliation

172. **Paranoia**: Irrational and persistent feeling of being persecuted or watched

173. **Delusion**: False beliefs held despite evidence to the contrary

174. **Obsession**: Persistent and intrusive thoughts or impulses

175. **Compulsion**: Repetitive behaviors driven by obsessive thoughts

176. **Fear**: Anxiety or worry about potential danger or harm

177. **Phobia**: Irrational fear of specific objects or situations

178. **Anxiety**: Persistent and excessive worry

179. **Panic**: Sudden, overwhelming fear or anxiety

180. **Terror**: Extreme fear or dread

181. **Dread**: Great fear or apprehension

182. **Alarm**: Sudden awareness of danger or trouble

183. **Worry**: Anxiety about potential problems or danger

184. **Unease**: Discomfort or anxiety

185. **Apprehension**: Fearful expectation or anticipation

186. **Timidity**: Lack of courage or confidence

187. **Cowardice**: Lack of bravery

188. **Submission**: Yielding to the authority or control of others

189. **Docility**: Ready compliance or submission

190. **Obedience**: Compliance with orders or requests

191. **Subservience**: Willingness to obey others unquestioningly

192. **Servility**: Excessive willingness to serve or please others

193. **Compliance**: Conforming to rules or standards

194. **Conformity**: Compliance with societal norms and expectations

195. **Acceptance**: Agreement with or belief in an idea or explanation

196. **Resignation**: Acceptance of something undesirable but inevitable

197. **Acquiescence**: Reluctant acceptance without protest

198. **Yielding**: Giving way to pressure or influence

199. **Submission**: Yielding to the authority or control of another

200. **Surrender**: Giving up resistance or control

201. **Capitulation**: Surrender under agreed conditions

202. **Compliance**: Conforming to a desire or command

203. **Obedience**: Compliance with an order or request

204. **Docility**: Willingness to be taught or led

205. **Inaction**: Lack of action or activity

206. **Lethargy**: State of being lazy, sluggish, or indifferent

207. **Indolence**: Avoidance of activity or exertion

208. **Laziness**: Unwillingness to work or use energy

209. **Slothfulness**: Reluctance to work or make an effort

210. **Negligence**: Failure to take proper care in doing something

211. **Carelessness**: Lack of concern or attention

212. **Inattentiveness**: Lack of attention

213. **Forgetfulness**: Failure to remember

214. **Absentmindedness**: Lacking in attention or concentration

215. **Distraction**: Diverting attention away from something

216. **Preoccupation**: Dominated by one thought or interest.

217. **Obsessiveness**: Excessive preoccupation with a single idea or activity

218. **Single-mindedness**: Focusing on one objective at the exclusion of others

219. **Fixation**: An obsessive interest in or feeling about someone or something

220. **Compartmentalization**: A form of psychological defense mechanism in which conflicting thoughts and feelings are kept separated or isolated from each other in the mind.

221. **Rashness**: Acting or tending to act too hastily

222. **Recklessness**: Lack of regard for the consequences of one's actions

223. **Thoughtlessness**: Lack of consideration for others

224. **Inconsiderateness**: Lack of thoughtfulness towards others

225. **Egotism**: Excessively conceited or absorbed in oneself

226. **Self-Absorption**: Preoccupation with one's own emotions or interests

227. **Self-Centeredness**: Concerned with oneself and one's own needs

228. **Narcissism**: Excessive self-love and self-centeredness

229. **Conceit**: Excessive pride in oneself

230. **Pridefulness**: An inflated sense of one's own worth

231. **Domination**: Exercising control or influence over others

232. **Supremacy**: The state of being superior to all others

233. **Exploitation**: Utilizing someone unfairly for one's own advantage

234. **Maltreatment**: Cruel or violent treatment of a person

235. **Mistreatment**: Ill-treatment or misuse

236. **Abandonment**: Leaving someone without support or care

237. **Desertion**: Abandoning a person or responsibility

238. **Estrangement**: Separation from social or familial relationships

239. **Alienation**: Feeling isolated or estranged

240. **Isolation**: Being separated from others

241. **Loneliness**: Sadness because one has no friends or company

242. **Desolation**: A state of complete emptiness or destruction

243. **Melancholia**: A severe form of depression

244. **Unhappiness**: The state of being unhappy

245. **Misery**: A state of great distress or discomfort

246. **Wretchedness**: A state of being very unhappy or unfortunate

247. **Helplessness**: Inability to act or react effectively

248. **Powerlessness**: Lack of ability to act or influence outcomes

249. **Defeatism**: Acceptance of defeat without struggle

OpenAI. (2024). *ChatGPT* [Large language model]. https://chatgpt.com

About the Author

I'm Miriam Matthews and I'm passionate about my God-given purpose to empower women towards their purpose! I am a wife, and mother of two girls and two boys. I became enthralled by this work after the "mystery" of my purpose was revealed and ignited through healing from pain and understanding the power of "my-story." As I began to shine my light, there were many that flocked to it.

My story encompasses the experience of a variety of traumatic experiences and God's goodness, and redeeming power. Prior to my transformation, I had a sense of worthlessness and immense self-doubt. I was a people-pleaser who would go with the flow. I would sabotage my goals at times, and lived a complacent life. I couldn't imagine doing great things because of my negative beliefs. However, as I began to understand God's love for me, it purified me and transformed me.

I realized that, as long as I looked at myself through the eyes of people, I would be disappointed. Many people are broken and they are simply projecting what is inside of them. Nevertheless, connecting with the Manufacturer who knew me before I was in my mother's womb, and who called me was key to understanding who I am and unlocking the power within me so I could be in my purpose.

I invested in my personal growth and hired my own coach. This was the best investment I have ever made, and there has been a huge return. Since we carry the DNA of Christ as His children, I had to take on the responsibility of defining my "DNA." This meant **diving** into my faith in God, **neutralizing** negative beliefs, and **activating** new powerful beliefs! The life you live will be as limited as your beliefs. Understanding who you truly are, and investing in your healing will literally transform your life and those connected to you.

I realized that there was a thief after my time and destiny because my destiny is great. Just like yours. That thief wants us to be confused about who we are because his job is to steal, kill and destroy, but I made a decision to receive life and life abundantly. This meant having the courage to leave behind my ways and go God's way. Jesus is the only way! When your way isn't working, it's time to turn to God's.

I am now both a licensed therapist and Christian transformational life coach! I enjoy helping women heal from the pain of their past, so they can activate their power and be in their purpose! As a result of my unique group coaching program, women have experienced deeper relationships with God, improved self-esteem, and clarity around their purpose. It has truly been an honor to be an integral part of each person's who and why. It's time for you to understand who you are, and why you were born! It's time to Define your DNA! Visit define-your-dna.com to learn more!

www.ingramcontent.com/pod-product-compliance
Lightning Source LLC
Chambersburg PA
CBHW020324130626
46549CB00003B/1002